World-Class In
Tales from my

Norman Marks

Table of Contents

Introduction 4

Chapter 1: In the beginning 6

Chapter 2: I am obdurate 10

Chapter 3: Too much quality 15

Chapter 4: The value of criticism 23

Chapter 5: The value of writing and teaching......................................26

Chapter 6: The value of curiosity and research 32

Chapter 7: The executive attention span...36

Chapter 8: You are how others see you...40

Chapter 9: The search for charisma 43

Chapter 10: The root cause..46

Chapter 11: Do we speak the same language? 52

Chapter 12: WIIFM...57

Chapter 13: Where do I go from here?..63

Chapter 14: Wearing a white hat 65

Chapter 15: Awkward days 70

Chapter 16: A great but unlikely compliment.....................................73

Chapter 17: When to suggest an answer 81

Chapter 18: Learning about limits 86

Chapter 19: Empathy 92

Chapter 20: The customer 99

Chapter 21: The best job I ever had...103

Chapter 22: Hiring the best...109

Chapter 23: Humility and respect 116

Chapter 24: The risk-based internal audit plan.................................119

Chapter 25: My first frauds 127
Chapter 26: Not all auditors hate risk 132
Chapter 27: Loretta and Wow! audit projects 137
Chapter 28: Why do I need to write an audit report? 144
Chapter 29: Auditing forward 156
Chapter 30: Effecting change 164
Chapter 31: Leadership 167
Chapter 32: Working with difficult people 175
Chapter 33: Working with a difficult region 184
Chapter 34: Organizational culture 191
Chapter 35: The expansion of internal auditing 200
Chapter 36: World-class internal auditing 209
Chapter 37: Celebrating mistakes 233
Chapter 38: Looking back and forward 237
Acknowledgments 239
About the Author 244

Introduction

I have never said that I was a world-class internal audit leader or that my team was world-class. I don't believe that anybody should presume to make that claim about themselves. It is arrogant and may well not only be wrong but an indication of complacency – that there is no need to change or seek improvement.

That doesn't mean that I am humble because I am very proud that many whom I hold in high esteem have put us on a pedestal. It is they who have said we were world-class.

Members of the audit committee said that when they think of the ideal internal auditor they think of me (which makes me uncomfortable), while executives said that "internal audit provides me with a competitive advantage", "your team has not performed an audit I wouldn't gladly pay for", "internal audit helps us stay efficient", and "Norman, you don't behave like an internal auditor".

I confess that the last is precious to me, coming from a curmudgeon of a senior vice president of human resources who started off laying down the law that internal audit was not welcome and had no value to her, but realizing after an operational audit that we had helped her solve a troubling organizational problem. Not only did she write a flattering letter of appreciation to my boss and his boss, but she let me drive her Cadillac!

In addition, my team and I have been profiled as innovators in the magazines of the American Institute of Certified Public Accountants and the (Global) Institute of Internal Auditors. When Protiviti (then Arthur Anderson) started to profile world-class internal audit departments, we were proud to be their first selection.

This book is a series of short stories about episodes from my professional life that gave me precious and enduring lessons. Taken as a whole, they explain who I am today and how I have practiced internal auditing as a chief audit executive for more than twenty years.

My hope is that these stories will amuse as well as provide some insights into how I came to lead internal audit departments as I did.

Maybe, and this is why I wrote the book, it will stimulate some thinking on your part.

If I have been recognized as leading world-class internal audit functions, it is because I have been extremely lucky to work with – and learn from – many world-class professionals. From audit committee members (including Wes Scott, Charlie Luellen, Greg Myers, Clarence Frame, Joe Ingrassia, Wayne Budd, Kurt Lauk, and so many more), to top executives (such as Tom O'Malley, Jay Allen, John Schwarz, C. S. Park, Joe Tang, Chester Lin, and more), to members of my audit and other teams (a list too long to mention here). Where I can I have paid tribute to them in each story and as many as I can remember are listed in the Acknowledgment section at the end of the book. My apologies in advance when I have forgotten to include individuals and mention their contribution.

Einstein said "A person who never made a mistake never tried anything new". I am no Einstein and I have made at least my share of mistakes – and some were huge! However, every mistake is an opportunity to learn. Many of these stories are about my mistakes and what I learned from them. If I share them with you, it is so that you will either not repeat them or will at least make smaller ones!

Now that I am retired, I am enjoying reliving these memories and I hope you find them of value.

Chapter 1: In the beginning

I joined the august public accounting firm of Cooper Brothers (which later became Coopers & Lybrand and is now PricewaterhouseCoopers) straight out of college. I was an "articled clerk", a throwback to the days when you learned a trade (in this case the auditing of public companies) as an apprentice to a master in the field. The term "articled clerk" refers to the articles of apprenticeship: the contract you signed with the firm. Traditionally, articled clerks paid their master; I was fortunate in that I received a small salary (£1,250 per annum) rather than the other way around!

Even though I had an accounting and finance degree from the London School of Economics, like all new hires I had to go through a few weeks of training in basic accounting and auditing. One of the sessions included watching a video made by the firm that was intended to show how the audit team functioned in the field, at the client's offices.

Imagine you are watching a team of three young men (the firm only hired women a year or two after I joined) reviewing accounting schedules. The door opens and in walks the manager. Pomp and circumstance! The manager removes and hangs up his bowler hat and gravely announces "Sorry for being late. I was held up at the bank!"

The trainees, including me, burst into laughter that was swiftly followed by a rebuke from our teacher. He informed us that the individual who played the part of the manager was not only a partner, but the son of the firm's managing partner! We should treat such gods with respect!

Over drinks that evening, my colleagues and I agreed that we would have to learn to show respect for the gods, even when they behaved like fools without realizing how silly they looked. It was absurd that not only did they not change the script, but the firm finished the video without changing the scene and continued to use it for several more years.

Later in the training course, our instructor had a moment of levity and told us a true story about the firm. Apparently, the partners had written a letter to the Lord Mayor of London congratulating the city on its anniversary. The writer added a paragraph that described how the firm had been a prominent part of the city since its founding in 1854; perhaps, he suggested, the city might recognize the firm by renaming the street on which it had its offices (Gutter Lane) as Cooper Lane.

The Lord Mayor wrote a formal letter in reply, noting that while the firm had a long and highly respected history dating back to 1854, the city and the street (Gutter Lane) had an even longer history that pre-dated the great fire of London in 1666. Perhaps, the Mayor suggested, the partners might consider renaming the firm as Gutter Brothers!

Pomposity, meet your match.

After a few more weeks, I was allowed to join the ranks of the auditors. In between audits, I was in the office studying for my Chartered Accountant's exam and became curious. I was working for an audit senior, who reported to a supervisor and then to a manager. But nobody had ever told me what title I had. What should I call myself if anybody (especially a girl) asked me what I did? So I went to that senior and asked him. He smiled at me and suggested I have a look at the "rate sheet" (a schedule that showed all the ranks, from partner on down, and what their standard hourly rate was). He told me that my position was listed at the bottom of the sheet.

I found one and read it. I saw partner, principal, senior manager, manager, supervisor, senior, semi-senior, executive secretary, secretary, copy typist, receptionist, and other. Yes. That was me at the bottom, below the copy typist and receptionist. I was an "other".

I could have been upset. Oddly, I was amused (I will admit to being jealous that the copy typists were paid more than me, a graduate of the LSE!) and have fun telling the story to this day.

I learned a valuable lesson from this. No matter how high you see yourself, how magnificent you look in the mirror of your vanity, others may see you as a pompous nitwit or worse.

∞

Another situation, many years later, reminded me never to think too highly of yourself.

As the new Vice President of Internal Audit of Solectron, I visited our Singapore offices. My regional audit director, Audrey Lee, was based there with her team.

My flight from San Francisco did not arrive until just after midnight local time, so Audrey was smart enough to tell me that she would pick me up at my hotel at about 10 am. She drove me to the office and as we got off the lift I asked her where I could get some coffee. I really needed it! She said, "But Norman, you have to meet Chester first!" I looked for a sign to the coffee as I asked her who Chester was. She told me that he was the President of Solectron Asia Pacific and he was waiting to see me.

Reluctantly, I let her take me in and introduce me to Chester. She took my bag and left to get coffee for me. Chester was a gracious gentleman and we talked for the best part of an hour.

I felt proud of myself for being able to talk business with a senior executive despite my jet lag, never having been in the region before, and only having a couple of months' experience in the business. I remarked to Audrey that I felt the meeting had gone well and that I had built the start of a good relationship with Chester.

She looked at me with amazement.

"Norman, Chester was speaking to you in Mandarin for the last twenty minutes!"

That put me in my place. Fortunately, Chester didn't realize it either and we did, in fact, have an excellent relationship. The incident didn't seem to affect Audrey, either; probably because I eventually woke up and we had some constructive conversations about the business and how we would run internal audit.

Respect is not the result of a title, or the fact you are the son of the managing partner and a partner yourself (whether you earned it or not), or a vice president from the home office.

No, respect is earned by your actions – and needs to be maintained and enhanced by continued excellence.

Chapter 2: I am obdurate

You learn things in the strangest ways.

After about a year with Coopers, I had worked on the audits of several companies under a number of audit seniors and supervisors. I felt that I had learned a great deal and my managers had told me they were pleased with my work.

So, when I was called in to meet with the group manager (a grey-haired individual who sat just below the gods) I was reasonably confident that I would get a decent performance appraisal. Let me tell you a little about him, to set the scene. Gordon, who I grew to like a great deal in future years, was a single male of about 50 who knew that he was never going to be a partner but had settled into the comfort of running a team of managers and staff of about 30 people. I had only met him once before, when I joined the group as a freshly-minted 'other'.

Now here I was, in the company of this nearly great man, to receive feedback on my performance. Gordon greeted me in a way that was more lukewarm than either formal or welcoming. I sat nervously and listened as he went through the early sections and explained that his comments were based on the feedback he had received from the seniors and supervisors I had worked for; he didn't have any personal observations since he had not supervised any of my work directly. The ratings were good, but somehow I knew that a bomb was about to be dropped.

He got to a section of the appraisal form where it asked about my ability to take direction. His tone changed slightly and he told me that I was below average and that I had been "obdurate". Fortunately, I knew what the word meant: stubborn, unwilling to change your opinion, and unmoved by persuasion. But I still asked Gordon to explain since I was surprised to hear this. He told me that he when he talked to my managers they told him that when they gave me directions I consistently asked questions rather than just doing what I was told.

This surprised me even more and I asked Gordon why this was a problem. None of my managers had said anything to me and I thought that the only way I would learn is by asking questions.

The bomb exploded.

Gordon told me that my behavior at the very moment was proving the point! I was being obdurate by not accepting the verdict of authority. My questions were an example of not being able to take direction and he believed the rating was correct and appropriate. His words and manner were stern and unforgiving.

I felt the pain, but was even after the blast unwilling to accept the verdict. How could asking my managers to explain what they wanted from me be wrong? Each of them had been very responsive and helpful, without any indication that what I was asking was inappropriate. So, I went to each of them and asked – and was relieved when they assured me that asking questions was not only appropriate but expected if I was to learn and progress. Gordon was, they said, an old school manager and had interpreted their comments in the context of his personal experience and bias that junior staff (apprentices) should be obedient and not question their masters. They also assured me that I was not 'obdurate'. Once I understood what was needed, I was able to follow directions and use my common sense and training to get the job done.

Over the years, I have continued to ask questions when I don't understand something rather than simply do what I was told. I believe very strongly that only when people have a solid understanding of why something needs to be done will they do it well.

That lesson applies in several ways. As auditors, we often ask why people do things the way they do. We don't accept the answers "because we have always done it this way," "because we were told to do it this way", or even "because the last set of auditors told us to do it this way." Those are not good answers; in all likelihood, they indicate that the work is not being done correctly.

As auditors, we should not fall into the same trap. When we rely on a checklist or last time's audit program to tell us what needs to be audited and what work needs to be done, we are doing what somebody else has decided is best in a different (even if similar) situation. A checklist is a useful reminder or way to test your own assessment. But it should never be followed without understanding what needs to be done and why, and questioning what it tells you to do.

Many years later, I was with a large savings and loan company (very similar to a mid-size domestic bank). After a few years in their internal audit department, leading among others the IT audit team, I had moved into IT management with responsibilities that included information security. Randy, one of my former IT auditors and a gentleman that I had hired and thought well of, was performing an audit of our information security program. He met with me to review his preliminary findings.

Randy told me that we had a serious control weakness in that we didn't change the phone numbers people used to dial into the data center. They needed to be changed at least once every quarter; otherwise there was a risk that over time the numbers would become known by hackers.

I agreed with Randy that changing the phone numbers reduced the risk that they would be compromised. However, as I pointed out, once somebody called the number they had to provide a userid and password. They were at the gate to the castle, but needed a key to open the front door. After three attempts, the userid was locked. In addition, changing the phone numbers frequently had three results: first, users would write them down and keep them in an easy-to-find location – a security issue; second, users would forget the number and be unable to do their work without calling the security help desk for assistance; and third, all of this carried a cost that was probably higher than the value of any risk reduction.

The risk reduction would be minimal because even after somebody was able to dial in, enter a valid userid and the correct password for that userid, they needed to get past additional security defenses. They had opened the front door of the castle but there were still a portcullis to navigate and additional doors to each of our systems and databases. The operating system (IBM's VM system) demanded a second userid and password. To enter an application, access a data base, or perform other functions, required at least one more – a third – access authorization.

I explained to Randy that the dial-up number was only the prelude to needing at least three additional levels of authorization before being able to steal data or damage our systems. In addition, I showed him an article about a tool used by hackers to automatically dial phone numbers until they detected the tone from a network modem – indicating a dial-up connection; the hackers could find out phone numbers even if we changed them! He agreed but said that changing the phone number was necessary.

By now, I was starting to lose my patience. I had hired Randy because he had a good combination of technical knowledge and common sense. Why couldn't he see that this was a silly recommendation? So I asked him why it was necessary.

Randy's answer: because a book by a notable IBM expert said you should change your dial-up phone numbers at least quarterly! Instead of using his common sense, he was relying upon advice from somebody who had no knowledge of our environment, the risks, and the costs.

I asked Randy to go back to his manager, a very experienced IT audit director who had been hired from outside the company to take my old job. Unfortunately, that individual told Randy to keep the point in. It was only taken out after the head of internal audit saw my response to the audit finding that explained how there was little to no risk but significant potential for business disruption and cost by changing phone numbers frequently. Incidentally, my manager (a senior vice president) and his manager (an executive vice president) were both quite concerned about the politics of disagreeing with an audit finding, but they trusted me to see it through.

A few years later, I joined Tosco Corporation as the head of internal audit, the start of some twenty years in that role. While I allowed the use of books, standard audit programs, and checklists as tools to remind auditors of areas to consider, I insisted that they were only a tool. Common sense, an understanding and appreciation of the business, and knowledge of risks and opportunities can never be replaced.

There is a magic word in the English language and it is 'Why'. It is a far more powerful tool than any checklist or book.

Chapter 3: Too much quality

I worked on a number of interesting audits during my time as a financial statement auditor. For example, one I was on early in my career was of a small manufacturing company. There were two of us on the audit, an audit supervisor (a position just below manager) and I.

One of my tasks was to see whether the trial balance (a list of the general ledger accounts and their balances) actually balanced. In other words, did the debits equal the credits. Now back in those days of yore, the general ledger was just that: a ledger book in which the accounts were maintained entirely by hand.

Of course, as my supervisor warned me, the trial balance did not balance. There were a number of errors that I was directed to correct through journal entries. But one stood out: what appeared to be a single-sided entry (i.e., an entry where only the debit or credit, but not both, was posted).

I talked to the company's Financial Director about the entry. I remember that when I went into the meeting I was a little intimidated. Here was a senior company executive, even if it was a small company. He ran the accounting function and reported to the Managing Director. He even had a company car!

The Financial Director told me that this was not a single-sided entry. He patiently explained that the business was actually two legal companies (company A and company B), each with its own general ledger. But only company B had a bank account. The journal entry was for a purchase of raw materials by company A, with a credit to cash and a debit to inventory.

I pointed out that the inventory was on the books of company A and the bank account in company B. He explained, again with patience, that was why he had credited cash on company B's general ledger and posted the debit to inventory on company A's books. When I explained that meant

15

that each would be out of balance, he didn't seem worried. He simply asked that I make the correction.

I left the meeting no longer intimidated. In fact, as I told my supervisor, I was stunned that the Financial Director – who even had a company car - didn't understand basic accounting and bookkeeping. He told me that he had known and all we could do was to get the books corrected and move on.

This taught me not to assume that individuals in authority or in positions that require specialized skills actually have the experience and ability they should. Sometimes this is because the people who hire and supervise them (the board or more senior executives) don't have the ability to detect the weakness; and, sometimes the individuals may misrepresent (e.g., on their resume) their experience and the Human Resources department doesn't do enough to check.

I had a different surprise on another audit, one of the first where I led the on-site audit team after my promotion to audit senior. The client was Hercules Powder Company (HPC), the UK subsidiary of an American multinational, Hercules Inc.

Before I get to the surprise, let me tell you about a curious and somewhat amusing incident.

For tax reasons, at the end of December HPC contracted with the Dutch division of Hercules Inc. to purchase a significant quantity of raw materials. It was an unusually large purchase that would meet the UK division's needs for a few months. The inventory was stored in Holland in a company warehouse owned by the Dutch firm, but was physically segregated while it was waiting for shipment. So, at year-end the UK division accounted for the purchase as inventory owned by them. This was correct according to UK accounting rules. However, according to

Dutch accounting rules the inventory needed to be recorded as owned by the Dutch division.

The value of the inventory was material to the financial statements of both divisions and the Dutch audit team (the local affiliate of our firm) advised us that they would have to issue a qualified audit opinion on the Dutch division's financial statements if they did not record the inventory as theirs. The Dutch audit team had a problem because the purchase was unusually large, very close to year-end, and the inventory had only been moved within the Dutch warehouse to a segregated location.

I discussed this with my manager who reviewed it with our partner. Their conclusion was that we (the UK firm) would have to issue a qualified audit opinion on the HPC's financial statements if the inventory was not recorded as owned by the UK division!

What a mess!

I wrote on behalf of the UK firm to the US audit team. They replied with the wisdom of Solomon: both the UK and Dutch divisions should record the inventory as owned by them, and the US parent would make an appropriate adjustment as part of the consolidation process.

This was a resolution that satisfied everybody.

Returning to the surprise, this was my third year as part of the audit team. I was assigned as a junior associate when Coopers was appointed auditor of Hercules Inc. My audit supervisor, a great mentor, was Kevin Gilbert. He taught me the value of using analytics, trends, and ratios as an audit technique. Hercules used a wide variety of chemicals in its manufacturing of an equally extensive number of products. Kevin developed a set of what we might now call metrics or performance indicators and used them to detect unusual patterns in inventory levels, margins, and so on. When combined with audits of the controls in key processes and physical inventory inspections, this was an effective method that kept the cost of the audit at a relatively low level.

I became fairly proficient in this technique and when Kevin was promoted (deservedly) to manager and I was appointed the senior in charge of the audit, I extended their use. Since I was very familiar with the technique and the rest of the team were able to follow Kevin's audit approach (the prior year workpapers were an excellent guide), we completed the audit with about 15% fewer hours than in the prior year!

The closing process also went very smoothly with just two exceptions: the first was the issue of the large purchase of inventory from the Dutch division. The other was that we had to finish our fieldwork and write the summary for the partner by candlelight! This was a time of union unrest in the UK, and the miners called a strike that left much of London without electrical power, including my team of auditors. Even though we were working late into the evening to complete the documentation by candlelight, we all stayed at our desks – although we did move closer to the windows so we could get a little illumination from the streetlights.

When I returned to the firm's offices at the end of the audit, I received a note from the group manager. Gordon directed me to take all the workpapers to the partner's office. The partner, Chris Lowe, wanted to review them. Now this was very unusual. Partners generally relied on the managers to review workpapers, but Gordon told me that Mr. Lowe wanted to see them. My guess was that he wanted to assure himself that all the work had been completed, because it was done so much faster than in the prior year.

I took them up to his office and left them with his secretary. Then I waited and waited, trying to be patient. I had confidence that all the work had been completed, but didn't feel good about the time the partner was taking to return them.

Eventually, I got them back with a note. Mr. Lowe wrote this:

"These are the best workpapers I have ever seen."

My heart leaped and a smile started to spread. But he continued:

"You spent too many hours on them."

Surprise!

My first reaction was confusion. I had completed the audit in record time and built nigh-on perfect workpapers in the process. Why was he complaining?

I asked Kevin. He sat me down and congratulated me for the praise part of the note. Then he explained what Mr. Lowe was saying.

Kevin told me that every hour spent on an audit was a cost and as a partner Mr. Lowe saw any extra hours as reducing his personal share of the firm's profits. While the quality of my work was commendable, it didn't need to be that good.

Kevin explained that the good far outweighed the negative and that Mr. Lowe was actually very pleased with the audit. However, the surprising criticism made a huge and lasting impression on me.

This experience led me to question the value of workpapers when I became a chief audit executive (CAE). While there is a clear need to document the work done as an external auditor (for protection in the event of litigation), the same need is not necessarily present for the internal auditor.

- The work of internal auditors is not reviewed by examiners or regulators, while external auditors' work is
- The opinion of the internal auditors, with the exception of government and similar environments, is for internal use only
- Internal auditors are rarely sued, whereas the external auditors may be sued by investors who rely on their published audit opinion
- While the International Standards for the Professional Practice of internal auditing require that there be evidence to support the internal auditor's assessment, they don't mandate working papers in the same way that external auditor standards do

There is value in working papers:

- If findings are disputed, the working papers provide evidence in their support. However, the facts behind audit findings are not often disputed; the debate with management, if there is one, is usually how to interpret the findings and assess the risk they represent
- Working papers are necessary if litigation is anticipated, such as in the case of a fraud investigation. This points to a need for working papers for investigations, but not for all internal audits
- Working papers enable a manager or supervisor review. However, most internal audit departments document in more detail than required for a manager to confirm the audit was completed to an appropriate level of quality. I prefer to review an audit by talking to the audit team, not by reviewing working papers
- Sometimes, reliance is placed on internal audit work by the external auditors. In those cases, documentation to a level agreed with the external auditors is required
- Sometimes, regulators or examiners (such as in banking or insurance) review internal audit work as part of their examination of the company. Working papers to agreed-upon standards are necessary

The key is to find a balance between the value of an audit engagement's working papers and the cost of creating them. (By the way, the cost of creating excessive working papers is not just the dollar cost of the staff and manager time. It is the opportunity cost: the opportunity to use those hours for another audit.)

Mr. Lowe believed that we were a little out of balance. With the benefit of hindsight and experience, he was correct.

Internal audit leaders need to ensure they have the right balance. A later incident heavily influenced my approach.

About 15 years after the Hercules audit, I was the head of internal audit at Tosco Corporation. Tosco was an oil refining and marketing company (more later) and I made a point of meeting with the internal audit departments of other oil companies to "benchmark" and compare practices. One of those companies was Atlantic Richfield (Arco), a much larger company than ours based in Los Angeles.

I met with the Arco managers separately from my meeting with the CAE. One of my questions was "what is the typical length of one of your audits?" The first part of the answer was not relevant to this story, but it is amusing: "the audit team spends as many hours as were budgeted". In other words, if they were able to finish early, they found a way to draw out the time. If the time budgeted was insufficient, they dropped areas from the scope of the audit. They used the example of an audit in Hawaii. It was usually budgeted for two weeks. If they finished the fieldwork in less time, they would move to the beach!

I shared that we used a technique called "stop and go auditing", where we would extend the audit if the risk was higher than expected and we needed more time to address it, but we would also cut short an audit if the risk was lower than anticipated. We always had more areas to audit than available resources, so if we could cut an audit short then the time we saved could be used for another audit.

Arco's second answer was that their average audit was about 1,000 hours in length. I asked why, because our typical audit was no more than 200 hours and I tried to keep most audits below 100 hours.

The Arco managers explained that an estimated 60% of their time was spent documenting their work for review.

There is no way that audit documentation should take such an enormous percentage of total time. If my internal auditors spent more than 10% of their time on working papers, I would need to know why.

These days, many departments have automated their working papers. However, I still have to question why they are spending scarce budget dollars on software to automate working papers. I suspect they are falling into the trap of documenting their audits because that is what they have always done (especially if they have never set aside their public accounting training), and the new software helps them do it in a consistent and, perhaps, less expensive way. It certainly does help when a manager wants to review working papers from his office without going to the audit location. But is that sufficient justification?

If we, as internal auditors, asked a business process owner "why are you doing this", would we accept the answer of "because we have always done it this way"? We would not. We would look to a valid business reason. The same holds for working papers: we should have a valid business reason for preparing working papers and for setting standards for them. That reason should balance the value and the cost (especially the opportunity cost) of working papers.

Chapter 4: The value of criticism

About a year later, I was a more experienced audit senior working on a large company audit. The on-site audit team was led by an audit supervisor with frequent visits by the audit manager. The manager assigned me the task of documenting and assessing the controls in the heavily-automated revenue and payables processes (we called them 'cycles' back then). The firm had issued new guidelines for flowcharting automated processes together with Internal Control Questionnaires (ICQs). I remember that they were a startling purple, compared to the ordinary light green of the traditional, manual controls-oriented ICQs of the past.

I told the manager that I hadn't seen these before and asked for his help. He replied that he hadn't seen them before either and that I should "figure it out". I was the best at this type of work (flowcharting and completing ICQs) on the team, and he was going to rely on me. So I read them all carefully and the examples that came with them.

It took me quite a while, but I got through the ordeal and felt pretty good. My manager had a look at my work and told me that the workpaper review would be performed by one of the firm's computer audit specialists. I have to admit I was concerned, because the Computer Audit Group (also known as CAG) was something of an elite unit, occupying a sacred space on the first floor of the London office. Still, I gave him the workpapers so he could pass them over.

A couple of weeks later, I received the workpapers back with a stack of review notes and a request to schedule a meeting with the CAG specialist. I opened the workpaper binder and saw red, literally. My beautifully-crafted flowcharts and completed ICQs were obliterated with red ink! (Yes, we did all of our work in ink in the UK in those days.) I can still remember thinking that there wasn't one question on the ICQs or one operation on any of the flowcharts that hadn't been criticized.

I read all the review notes and had to admit that they all made sense. It was not a good feeling to recognize that the red ink was deserved and not at all unfair!

I arrived at the scheduled meeting and was greeted by a gentleman who introduced himself as a CAG Supervisor (Jarlath). He launched in and told me that my workpapers were some of the worst he had ever seen, that my poor effort had wasted a lot of his time (clearly worth much more than mine), and he wondered whether I had learned anything at all from the 3 days of training I had taken.

"Three days of training?" I said. "I didn't get any training at all. I was given the forms and told to do the flowcharts and answer the ICQs."

His face showed his astonishment and his tone changed to concern. He asked me to confirm that I hadn't received any training, which I was pleased to do.

We then spent a productive couple of hours as he essentially trained me by reviewing what I had done, explaining why it was wrong, and showing me what I should have done. I left invigorated and went back to my desk to redo the entire set of workpapers.

Did I get them totally correct the next time? No. But the number and level of review comments was at an acceptable level and easy for me to address.

My manager heard about the level of review comments and was quite critical. He told me that I had not represented either myself or the team well and the hours I had spent on the work were excessive. Frankly, I thought his criticism was unfair but I had learned my lesson and accepted it (while simmering inside).

I was a good auditor, understood the basic business processes, and had respectable flowcharting skills. But I didn't understand the fundamental principles behind my task. I had neither training nor experience on which to base my documentation and assessment of the computer controls within the revenue and payables business processes.

Over the years, I have come to learn that if you are to be effective in any position you have to have a solid grasp of the fundamental principles. If you have that understanding, you have a firm foundation on which to add technical and other skills and build expertise you can rely on.

Coming back to the criticism.

Jarlath gave me constructive, fair, and clear criticism that helped me not only fix what was wrong but understand why it was wrong. The latter was critical and I am grateful to this day for it. He criticized my work and not me as a person. Although at first his tone was harsh, when he realized I hadn't received the training that I was supposed to have received, he became as much a teacher as anything else.

The criticism didn't hurt; it educated and changed me.

Two postscripts are of note.

A few months later, I received a message from the CAG group. They offered me a place on their team starting in January. Apparently, Jarlath had told his manager that given I had zero training, I had in fact done quite well. My second effort had even impressed him. I accepted the offer and haven't looked back.

Two years later, as a CAG manager, I was asked to work with a manager from the New York office on a project to develop the global firm's approach to data center audits (see Chapter Six). My manager introduced me to the US team member, who turned out to be……………. Jarlath (who had no memory of reviewing my work!)

Chapter 5: The value of writing and teaching

I never received good grades at school when the subject required me to write, whether we are talking about high school or university. I love History but my teachers had no affection for my essays about Gladstone and Disraeli. I adore the French language, country, cuisine, and people. But I was far better speaking in French than writing in that language. We won't discuss how poorly I fared in English Literature!

So, when I was asked to write about advances in technology and how that would affect our clients and audit practice, I tried to weasel my way out.

A little background: after I joined CAG, I attended 5 weeks of off-site training. The first part was led by Honeywell and they taught us computer programming in general and COBOL in particular (in those days, few learned any programming at college). For whatever reason (perhaps because I was a serious chess player), I found I had a facility for programming in general and COBOL and the firm's audit software (something called AuditPak) in particular. I also performed reasonably well in the second part, where we talked about internal controls in 'computerized' applications (i.e., business processes that relied heavily on computer applications).

During the last week of the off-site, the CAG senior manager (David Clark) pulled me aside and asked me to be the group's 'technical' expert. I must have looked at him with stunned eyes and I recall reminding him that I hadn't even completed the training! He agreed that it was unusual to ask somebody with zero experience to be an expert, but that the Honeywell lead said I was "the most gifted programmer he had trained" (to this day, I have a hard time believing such hyperbole) and the managers leading the computer auditing sessions had told him I was among the best on those topics as well. David believed I could do a fine job and described the responsibilities as being a resource when staff members had problems with their programming (a large part of the CAG workload was writing software to help the financial auditors). He also wanted me to help him and the rest of the team stay abreast of new technology.

How could I refuse such a vote of confidence from one of the CAG gods?

For the first couple of months, I was rarely asked to act as an 'expert'. I was assigned a number of clients where I performed computer audit assignments such as writing software to help in the audit of the financial statements, documenting and assessing the controls in computerized applications, and running test data to test complex calculations in those applications.

Then, David asked me to come into his office.

After the customary pleasantries, he said he wanted me to develop a program where I would learn about new technology, determine how it would affect our client's businesses and our audit of their financial statements, and then share that information with the rest of CAG. I had a small budget so I could attend seminars, etc. and subscribe to appropriate technical journals.

One of the first expeditions I took into the land of new technology involved attending a series of sessions on data bases at the British Computer Institute. I heard about all kind of data base structures, schemas, sub-schemas, and more. It was fascinating and I was starting to worry about translating this to the rest of CAG. What did it mean to our clients, their business processes, and our audit approach?

The last session was memorable. The presenter was Tom Gilb. Tom is an American that moved to the UK as a teenager (but kept his accent and sense of humor), spent most of his working life as a consultant, has written several technical books, and is an Honorary Fellow of the British Computer Society.

More to the point for me was that he was an engaging speaker. He took the highly technical and spoke about it in plain English.

Tom told his rapt audience about an engagement he had with a Scandinavian car company. They wanted a fully integrated system, running against a single (although large and complex) data base, that tied in customer orders, procurement, factory planning, inventory management, fulfillment, billing, and accounting. This was something that, to his knowledge, had never been done.

The client talked to IBM and purchased their most powerful computer; if memory serves me right, it was an IBM 360 mainframe running the DOS operating system, the CICS transaction processing system, and an early version of the IMS data base system. Tom told us that IBM assured his client that this was sufficient power to run the massive system.

The software was developed, the data base designed and populated, and testing started. Each module (customer order processing, receivables, factory planning, etc.) was tested and found to be working well.

Then, they tested the integrated system. That did not work as well. They input about an hour's volume of customer orders, and they appropriately updated inventory management, created the necessary purchase orders, were considered in factory planning, led to correct billing upon completion and delivery, and the appropriate entries in the financial records.

Unfortunately, that hour's volume took more than 24 hours to process all the way through the system!

The lesson, as Tom explained, was that the design of the data base was critical but the designers of the overall, integrated system were overly optimistic – as was IBM. Rather than trying to integrate all these various pieces in one ambitious project, they should have done it in stages. When using new technology, the company should learn its capabilities and limitations before taking a giant leap forward. The mistake cost the company several millions and delayed upgrades to the existing system for many months.

Tom talked about the need to understand the fundamentals and build new systems and applications on a solid foundation. The client was so focused on the advertised potential that they forgot basic and fundamental principles of technical application and file design. They should have been able to calculate the demand that such massive integration would place on the new hardware and operating system, and predict that it was beyond its capabilities.

They also believed that moving from traditional stand-alone files to data base was a magic pill that would make everything possible.

Tom shot that down with magic words of his own: he told us that data base was "just another file structure" and that the basic principles that all computer engineers had learned about file design still applied.

The lesson I learned and applied throughout my career was that while technology, organization design, and other practices might change, most of the underlying principles remain the same. If you understand the primary and foundational principles of management, auditing, internal controls, risk management, information security, cash management, and so on, you will do well even in the midst of massive change. But if you don't have a solid foundation, you are building a castle in mid-air.

David made me write a paper so everybody else could understand data base and what it might mean to them. I was able to use my experience auditing the Guardian Royal Exchange (a large insurance company), as they also used an IMS data base system and part of my work had been writing software against their system. I understood what data bases were, could talk about them, had real life examples to share, and believed I would explain them to the rest of CAG. In fact, it only took me about half-a-dozen drafts and rewrites before I was able to produce something that satisfied (if not pleased) David.

My next adventure took me into a new and smaller world: the world of microprocessors.

People I knew were buying do-it-yourself microcomputer 'kits' from mail order stores, and the technical computing journals were starting to hint that these devices had the potential to move from a hobby to a business tool. In 1974, a company called Zilog was founded and in 1976 they introduced the Z80, an 8-bit microprocessor that was a significant advance from the early Intel 8080 model. The Z80 allowed more powerful devices and the military, in particular, used it extensively. The Z80 powered early business computers, such as the Osborne, Kaypro, Xerox 820, Radio Shack TRS 80, and Amstrad. I purchased a Radio Shack TRS 80 Model II a little later – but that's another story.

I believed in the potential and wanted to share that vision with the rest of CAG. After obtaining materials directly from Zilog and accumulating a number of pieces from journals, I started to write. I was smart enough to include diagrams, but not smart enough to please David with the initial drafts of my paper.

After I had exhausted my patience and wanted to give up, and David had nearly exhausted his patience with me, he gave me two pieces of sage advice:

1. Tell him (in person) why this is important. Say it and then write what you said. As you are saying it, learn from the listener (David) how to express your thoughts in a way that will be understood – and learn what not to say because it will not be understood.
2. Avoid technical language and use ordinary English where possible. If you have to be technical, explain the terms clearly so that the non-technical person will understand.

I ended up writing a much longer piece, but it worked. While not everybody would share my opinion of the potential, everybody understood what I was talking about.

Later that year, I was asked to be one of the teachers at the off-site training session for people joining CAG. This was a wonderful learning experience for me. The task of teaching meant that I had to master the fundamentals of what I needed to teach. It was also essential that I avoided technical language when plain English could be used – and that I explain the technical in easy-to-absorb-and retain terms.

This set of experiences led me to require all of my staff to:

- Write and speak for the people who are listening, the people you are trying to influence, inform, or persuade
- Write and say what they need to hear, rather than what you want to say
- Use language they understand. If they don't start with a decent understanding of the topic, explain any technical terms in ways they can understand
- Give examples and use diagrams; they are of great value in expressing ideas, especially to those who are visually oriented (i.e., absorb concepts from seeing better than they do by reading). I became used to getting up and using a chalkboard to diagram and explain what I was trying to communicate
- Master the fundamentals: you won't get far explaining anything unless you have deep understanding of the topic yourself

Chapter 6: The value of curiosity and research

One of my first clients as a computer auditor was a large insurance company in the north of England: the Guardian Royal Exchange (GRE). This was a major account, with significant computer audit work in support of the financial statement audit.

My first assignment was to run "test data" that was designed to provide assurance that the reserve for incurred but not received claims (IBNR) was reasonable. The IBNR calculation was complex, too complex for any manual recalculation or simulation through audit software. So another test method was needed. Some years earlier, a test routine was developed that involved running the IBNR software against data created by the auditor. The auditor had calculated what the IBNR reserve should be for this relatively small set of data. If the results of running the test data against the IBNR software were consistent with the auditor's calculation, the IBNR software could be considered as working as desired.

I followed the instructions for running the test data routine, documented in an audit program. It involved talking to the IT staff to update the run instructions (Job Control Language, or JCL), then giving them the combined test data and JCL deck. (In those days, we were using punch cards.)

When the results came back, I reviewed them to confirm that the correct test deck and JCL had been used. I also reviewed the IBNR calculation and verified that it was consistent with the predetermined expected results.

Everything was as it should be – at least on the surface. But something seemed strange.

Being the curious person that I am, I had picked up an IBM manual or two to read while I was waiting for meetings. One was on a topic called the Linkage Editor. (I will explain how that software works later, as part of another story). For now, it's enough to know that it helped me see that something was strange in the test data run. One of the files used in the run had been read from a tape drive (usually used for files taken from storage) instead of run from disk (which is where current programs and files resided).

I met with the IT manager who had been assigned by the company's head of IT to work with the audit team. He reviewed the results with me and told me that everything was fine.

"Norman, we did what we always do for you. We loaded the IBNR software that was used in the original audit test, five years ago, and ran your test data through it. What you see as being loaded on a tape drive is the archived copy of the IBNR software."

Oh. I asked why an archived copy of the IBNR software had been used instead of the current programs used to calculate the IBNR reserve we were auditing – but as I was framing my question, the answer was becoming clear in my mind. By the time he replied, I knew what he was going to say.

"But Norman, we have been updating the IBNR software constantly. The test data that your man put together five years ago won't work with today's software. We knew that, so we carefully preserved the code he used so your test would work."

So, for five years the CAG team had been running a worthless test. If the auditor had understood exactly how the test data was being run, he should have been able to see what was (or was not) happening. Only my curiosity and delving into the IBM manual led me to recognize that something was wrong.

Obviously, I updated the test data and developed an audit program that would not only work that year, but in future years as well.

It may have been this incident that sparked a life-long interest in what we now call IT general controls, but back then we called data center controls.

I was back the next year, this time as the manager of the CAG team; I had assigned myself the task of reviewing the data center controls.

In those days, little was known by computer auditors about the potential for the systems programmers (the most technical of the IT staff, they maintained the operating system, data base software, and so on) to affect the operation of enterprise applications. Pretty much all we knew was that they had the ability to use so-called "utility" programs that had enormous power: they let the systems programmers make changes to data or to application code, bypassing any controls. The most famous were the "ZAP" family of products (used in the IBM environment). There were variations for the different operating systems, but in the GRE environment, the one we were concerned with was "SuperZap" (sometimes referred to as SPZAP).

We had a step in the data center controls audit program to assess whether the company had sufficient controls over SuperZap. According to the prior year's audit file, the company had determined that they needed to make SuperZap available to systems programmers only in the event of an emergency. So, they had "hidden" the program by renaming it to something only known to the head of IT. If there was an emergency, the head of IT would rename SuperZap and provide that new name to the systems programmer. When it was no longer needed, the head of IT would hide it again by renaming it.

I had been working with these systems programmers on some audit software (which I was running against the company's IMS database, so I needed their technical support). I had a high opinion of their abilities and doubted that the IT director, who was not a technician but had a background as a COBOL programmer, could realistically hide it from them.

I got a copy of the IBM manual that explained SuperZap. In one of the very first paragraphs, it described how the utility could be executed either by its file name, AMASPZAP, or through aliases (literally, other names). The most common alias is IMASPZAP.

I wondered. OK, my firm's computer auditors had been fooled (innocently, I assumed) into thinking that the test data run was a test of the software used to calculate the IBNR reserve. Had the IT director also been fooled?

I stopped by his office and asked him if SuperZap had been renamed to IMASPZAP. His jaw dropped and he asked me how I knew. After I explained that IMASPZAP was a standard alias that was described in the IBM manual and probably known to every one of his systems programmers, his jaw snapped back and his teeth clenched. He agreed to change the way in which SuperZap (however named) was to be controlled.

This taught me to look a little deeper and make sure that I really understood what I was being told. This story is about my time as a computer auditor and is somewhat technical. But the same thing applies to other areas of auditing, such as compliance with regulations. Too few people actually read the regulations, the underlying laws, or commentary on related litigation.

Later, I found out that the IT director told the engagement partner that I was head and shoulders above any previous computer auditor he had worked with – internal or external. My little demonstration of common sense (on the test data) and desire to understand what I was looking at (the utility program) impressed him. Over the years, I have had similar experiences where a smidgeon of common sense and technical knowledge (in each case obtained by reading and research) turned a skeptical manager ("auditee") into a trusting and valued partner of internal audit.

Chapter 7: The executive attention span

After a year or so, David called me into his office. He had noticed my interest in data center controls and that I was pressing for more caution in reviewing what the systems programmers were doing. At that time, there was little appreciation (reflected in our audit programs) of the risk; these people had the ability to make changes to many elements of the computer environment that could affect financial reporting: changes directly to data files; changes to application programs – even while they were running in memory; changes to the data base management system; and, changes in the operating system. I had drafted a supplemental internal control questionnaire (ICQ) to address these risks, which a few others were starting to use.

David told me that the global firm (which was now Coopers & Lybrand, or C&L) had decided to review its approach to the audit of controls at data centers. A senior person from the US firm would take the lead and the other, representing the 'rest of the world', would be me.

The senior person from the US firm turned out to be Jarlath (see Chapter 3) and we met a few weeks later. It had been decided that we would call the controls at data centers "Integrity Controls". This was not my choice, and in today's rearview mirror it is clearly a misleading term. The equivalent in today's language is "IT general controls", but for the moment let's use "Integrity Controls".

Jarlath and I were an effective team. We discussed and agreed on the broad principles, then he went back home to New York and I stayed to do all the work. He was a very effective delegator! Frankly, I didn't mind, as I was able to write everything my way. It also gave me a great opportunity to think about how these processes worked, whether and how they represented a risk, and how we should not only understand the controls but how they could be audited.

During the period, I was walking towards my office when David called out to me. He was speaking to one of the most exalted of the gods: the senior partner in charge of the UK firm's computer audit activities. Brian Jenkins was an imposing figure. Standing about 2 feet taller than me (or so it seemed; it was probably just a few inches), the future Sir Brian Jenkins, Lord Mayor of London, had a deep baritone voice of immense authority. I had heard him speak but had never been within 20 feet of him until David called me over.

Mr. BGJ (we called all the partners by their initials) greeted me in a friendly way. He said that David had told him I was working on the Integrity Controls project and asked me how it was going.

I collected my thoughts and started to reply – only to notice that his attention had wandered off. I have no idea where it went. Maybe he was thinking about the great deeds he would perform when he got back to his office. I don't know. All I did know was that while his ears may have been hearing what I was saying, his mind was not listening.

I found my way to the end of my report, said it was nice to meet him, and cringed my way to my office – now definitely 2 feet smaller.

I saw David return to his office and followed him in. He saw my face and confirmed that Mr. BGJ had stopped paying attention to me as soon as he saw me hesitate.

David, one of the finest mentors you could ask for, explained that people like Sir Brian have no patience. They need to hear answers to their questions straight away, in a clear and succinct voice.

Executives like him "have the attention span of a gnat".

I have used that expression ever since and taken its lessons to heart.

When communicating with senior executives, whether in management or on the board, they need you to get to the point quickly, communicate what they need to know and no more, and then answer their questions in the same manner. They don't want to be bothered by stuff they don't need to know.

This style of communication extends beyond the oral to the written.

I learned two lessons from this very brief encounter with a god:

1. Effective executives have an immense amount on their plate and want to spend as little time as possible on every topic, so they have little or no patience with people who waste their time with trivia – information the executive doesn't need to know
2. When we communicate with the gods of our world, we need to tell them what they need to know, rather than what we want to say. Too often, we want to share details that show how good our work was, which is important to us, when all the executive really needs to know was our conclusion and whether they need to do anything

This translates into every communication we make with senior management. How can we get to the point as quickly as possible, and provide the information with the clarity needed so they can take the actions we desire?

Over the years, I learned that there is an immense difference between what we would like to say, to demonstrate we have done quality work and reached important conclusions, and what executives need to hear.

In this case, I wanted to show the great man that I was confident in the task, I was working well with my US counterpart, that we were making good progress, and he could have confidence in us. In contrast, he wanted only to know whether we were on track and whether there were any issues he could help with. He was also using the opportunity to size me up, to assess whether David had assigned a competent individual to the project.

The typical internal auditor wants to demonstrate that the work was thorough, according to standards, and that the conclusions and recommendations are supported by credible evidence. The executive wants to know whether there are issues he should be aware of, how critical they are to his objectives, and what he needs to do about them.

This leads the internal auditor to write an essay when all the executive needs is a punch line.

The auditor writes a 10 page report with a one or two page executive summary, just to say that with the exception of one item (which is being appropriately addressed by management) everything is fine.

∞

A test I like to give my people is to imagine that they are boarding an elevator on the 3rd floor that has the CEO inside. He asks "what do I need to know about your audit?" The auditor has until the elevator reaches the ground floor to answer. I used this technique when I joined Solectron as CAE and was reviewing a draft audit report from Singapore following an audit of the factory in Shenzhen, China. The audit report format was excellent in many ways, with a dashboard on the first page that had separate lines for each of the major areas and a 'traffic light' (i.e., red, tallow, or green) indicating whether the controls in the area were effective. But when I looked at that first page on this particular report, all I call see was red. Every risk area was red.

I called the Singapore team director (Audrey Lee) and asked her what the report meant, being all red. Her reply was that it meant the controls were poor. I asked what that meant to the business; she didn't know how to answer, so I gave her the elevator question. What would she tell the CEO as the elevator descended? I asked her to call me back the next day with her answer.

When she called back, she told me that "the processes and controls in Shenzhen will not be able to support the planned 20% growth in production".

This was a meaningful conclusion, relevant to the business and useful to the executives. We made it the first thing the readers of the audit report would see. Then they could go to the detail for why we felt that way.

Chapter 8: You are how others see you

Completion of the Integrity Controls project led to a significant increase in my reputation, my standing in the computer audit team around the world, and in my self-confidence. So, when I joined David in his office to receive my annual evaluation I was expecting it to be good.

Certainly, David had many nice things to say about my work on the Integrity Controls project, on client engagements, and my support of the team as the 'technical expert'.

However, he then told me that I had a problem. I would not be able to advance if I continued to upset senior managers. I asked what he meant and he explained that he had received feedback from the senior manager in charge of one of the Northern England office, a peer of David's. This senior manager thought that I was arrogant and didn't show him sufficient respect. David said that he understood that as the more technical person and the expert on Integrity Controls, people were coming to me for advice and guidance. But, especially when they are more senior to me I must be careful to show them respect – even when what they say doesn't deserve it.

I found it very difficult to understand what David was telling me. I always felt somewhat intimidated by authority and couldn't recall a single instance when I had behaved with anything but respect towards this senior manager. David told me that while almost anything except subservient behavior was likely to appear arrogant to this individual, he had seen me behave in a way that might be perceived as arrogant in other settings.

Let me skip ahead a moment and tell you that after I left David I spent a fair amount of time by myself, thinking about what he had said. Arrogant? I couldn't see it. So, I spoke privately to some of my co-workers, people I trusted, and asked them whether they thought I ever behaved arrogantly. I was shocked to hear that yes, at times I did seem to hold myself in great esteem with those around me somewhat less capable. They shared some examples and promised to let me know if they ever saw me behave that way again.

People tell me I am smart, even that I am the most significant thought leader in internal audit. What I keep reminding myself is that however smart I may be, there are many smarter than I am – and my excellence (if true) is in a narrow area. This saying has been attributed to people like Socrates and Confucius, and I quote and remind myself of it all the time:

"A wise person knows the limits of their knowledge and the vast extent of their ignorance."

Showing that you are the best at what you do may win you a job, but will rarely win friends or influence people. If we are to be successful, we need to surround ourselves with people who are interested in our success as well as their own. Arrogance turns them away.

This is especially true for internal auditors. They will often hear an explanation from somebody whose area they are auditing that makes no sense. For example, I have heard a board chairman (no less) say that his company had little risk of financial statement fraud because they only hired honest people! That is absurd, but the auditor needs to remember always to show respect and never the scorn he or she may feel inside. You will never get the respect you want, or influence change as effectively as you desire, if you don't show respect to others – even if they don't seem to deserve it.

There's another attribute that you need to be successful, and David shared it with me during my review:

> "Norman, you don't have any charisma. You made some friends in the States with your work on Integrity Controls. Maybe you can arrange an exchange with them [an exchange is where the UK sends somebody to work for a while in the US and the US sends somebody to work in the UK]. They have more charisma than they need and maybe some of it will rub off on you!"

What could I say? Nothing.

It is important to know how others see you, and I always try to find a way. I ask my manager, my peers, and my staff. I listen and if I don't like what I hear I do what I can to change. David was telling me, bluntly, that I needed to move from being a technical expert to being a more charismatic leader.

Chapter 9: The search for charisma

I won't say that I was able to steal charisma from the Americans, but I was able to arrange an exchange with them. The deal was that I would work in their Atlanta office for six months (which was extended at their request for another three months in the national office in New York). In exchange, the London office would host, a few months later, a manager from Philadelphia.

During that time, I worked with a number of charismatic individuals. Stan Halper, the leader of the US computer audit practice, was a dynamic and inspirational leader. When you worked for him, he truly loved you and you knew it. But if you disappointed him he could be loud and vulgar. I was in his office one time when he was on a call with a manager who had not met Stan's expectations. Stan didn't just yell and scream obscenities, he threw the phone across the room where it broke into pieces. He then turned to me and smiled a welcome.

I loved Stan and it was very sad that when he passed away very few of his team attended the funeral. I didn't find out until later, as we lost touch after I left the firm, but would have tried to be there for the great man.

Another was Glenn Davis. He was Jarlath's friend and manager, and I met him on the Integrity Controls project. Glenn was the epitome of smooth and charismatic, with the biggest and warmest smile you can imagine. It made you want to please him. He later rose in the ranks to senior partner with Coopers & Lybrand.

The group manager in charge of the Atlanta and other offices in the region (such as Birmingham, Alabama, and Memphis Tennessee) was Norm Stratton. Norm could turn on the charm, but not as well as the senior manager in charge of Atlanta, Tom Farrell. Tom always seemed in control and unflappable. I found him friendly and I trusted him. But, he didn't have the same capacity to pull you in and want to make him proud of you as Stan and Glenn.

Some of this must have rubbed off on me, because I don't hear about a lack of charisma any more. I have tried to make an adjustment that doesn't change who I am. I have found that you have to be true to yourself, but that doesn't mean you can't learn to smile – a big smile – that is not limited by shyness. Charisma is behaving in a way that others find appealing. A smile that acknowledges and shows warmth will create a difficult-to-resist urge to smile in return.

I have also learned that not only do we need to recognize that we only succeed through the efforts of others, but the value we place on those individuals must be shown to them in every interaction. People respond when they believe you respect them.

My nature is somewhat shy and introspective. But I have learned that pretty much everybody I will ever meet is valuable and interesting in one way or another. Not only are people interesting as individuals and have much to teach me, but they often have perspectives, experiences, and insights that are different and therefore interesting. My view of this world and my small place in it has been enlightened by conversations about all kinds of topics with all manner of people around the world.

When it comes to business, managers and executives are not the only people with information and insights of value. Tom Peters said that if you want to know what is really happening in an organization, you should talk to the janitor. Why, because managers only think they know what is happening. That is why internal auditors are needed, to explain to managers and executives that what they think is happening is really not.

If we are to understand the business, we need to listen to people from managers to floor sweepers, from the people who talk to the customer (whether in sales, managing a store, or staffing a help desk) to those who develop strategy, from those who work in the warehouse to those in charge of procurement, and from the CIO to the staff responsible for software testing and quality control.

I have learned that people love those who will listen to them. You can be charismatic by listening actively, showing respect and attention to another's views.

In fact, I tell people that I don't want them ever to "go and talk to somebody". I want them to "go and listen". If they are talking more than half the time, they are not listening effectively and learning what the other person has to tell them – and they will not only be the poorer for that, but will have less influence with that person in the future.

I think of charisma, as David was using the term, as this: "a personal quality that makes a person capable of inspiring or influencing others". I have learned that listening, showing respect, valuing others, and demonstrating ability through action, not just words, gives you the power to inspire and influence.

Chapter 10: The root cause

I had a number of interesting assignments while I was in Atlanta. The one that made the greatest lasting impression was at the long distance division of the telephone company AT&T, AT&T Long Lines. My task was the integrity controls audit of their data center just to the north of Atlanta.

A junior associate and I reviewed and assessed the data center's operating procedures. They were thorough and met all our expectations. We moved on to testing the controls.

C&L (US) had purchased a software programming language (I will refer to it as CA2) and was using it to develop an "SMF Analyzer" software tool. AT&T used IBM mainframes and operating systems; IBM's "SMF" (System Management Facility) refers to what is essentially a log of activity on the system. When the operator starts a "job" (i.e., a set of instructions to run a program), a record is written to SMF. When that job starts a program, another record is written. When the job opens a file, another record is written – distinguishing whether the file is opened so it can be read, updated, or written. At the end of the job, another record is written that indicates whether the job ran to successful completion or not (a failure is called an "abend" or abnormal termination).

Since I had some experience in the UK using a fairly primitive analytics tool against SMF data, I was encouraged to use the more powerful US tool for the AT&T audit. The value is that by mining SMF data you can build what is essentially an audit trail, then select activities such as program changes for testing.

The firm had only recently acquired the tool and what I was given to start with was rudimentary at best. However, the language was easy to learn and use and the IBM manuals on SMF were excellent. So, I spent a lot of my work and free time developing a fairly complete set of programs. For a defined period, they identified changes to existing programs (by identifying changes to production program libraries); the addition of new programs; as well as what jobs were run, the files they updated, and whether they ran to a normal termination or abended. I was able to recreate what amounted to the full JCL deck for any job that updated a production data file.

I selected a number of program changes for testing: looking to see whether the change was tested and approved by both IT and user management. A surprising number of changes that only had IT management approval and I could not find any record of testing. The IT approval was by less senior people than required by AT&T's normal procedure. I asked IT management about it and they told me they were emergency changes. When a program failed during overnight production processing, the responsible programmer would make a change to the code, test it, and after approval from the IT Operations Supervisor, the revised program would be moved into production and run.

All the program changes I was looking for were logged as emergency changes and had been approved by the IT Operations Supervisor. As there was no record of testing, I started writing up an item for the audit report recommending tightening the controls over emergency changes. For example, the procedure for emergency changes had not been formalized and approved by senior IT management.

I was also looking at how management responded to production jobs that abended. When a production job failed, that could mean a failure to update accounts, bill customers, and so on. So it was important that management monitored and took appropriate action when there was a production abend.

I found that a large number of production jobs were failing. Sometimes, they were run again only to fail again. I talked to a few people in operations and heard that the high number of changes was due to the high number of production failures. The high number of production failures, in turn, was due to the high number of emergency changes, made and tested by swamped and tired programmers coming in at night several days in a row, which then failed in production. While the programmers may have been diligent at first, as they lost more and more nights' sleep to come in to fix their failed fixes, they became more interested in finishing work and getting back to bed.

I drafted an audit comment to this effect and shared the results with my managers. The issue was escalated to the manager and partner of the overall audit, who talked to senior company management in New Jersey. To nobody's surprise, management had no knowledge of this state of affairs and challenged my finding. I provided the details and waited for them to investigate using their own tools.

But I didn't sit on my hands while I was waiting. I had a feeling, perhaps it was my common sense talking to me, that the current level of production failure, emergency change, and subsequent production failure didn't happen overnight. There had to have been a steady build-up. I wrote a new program that provided a report of production failures by month for the last several months. It showed not only a progression, but that the rate of growth in the level of failures was close to logarithmic!

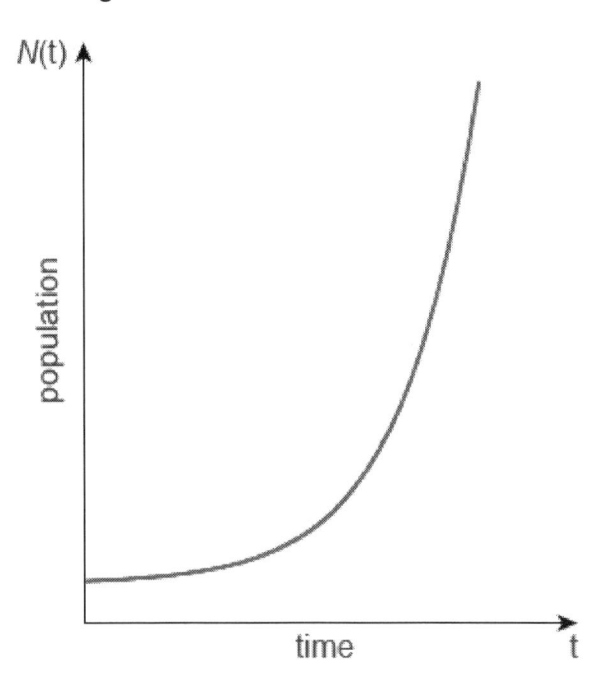

When management saw the chart and was able to obtain confirmation from their own IT managers that my data was correct, they moved quickly to act.

Fortunately, I was able not only to show the current situation and the risk it presented to the business, but indicate the root cause: a less than disciplined approach to the testing and approval of emergency changes to production programs. Management slowed down the implementation process for emergency changes, not only to ensure a more disciplined process but also to make sure that the people making the changes were able to do so while fresh.

If the auditor reports a problem that is only a symptom, management is unlikely to take the actions necessary to fix the problem permanently. Only when the root cause is treated, rather than the symptom, is the deficiency addressed.

∞

I have learned over the years that there is a powerful word in the English language: Why. When the auditor sees a situation that is questionable, he or she should ask why it happened. But it may take as many as six "why" questions before you get to the root cause. For example, consider this scenario:

> Auditor to accountant: "I see that the account reconciliations are not up to date. In fact, they are several months old. Why is that?" #1
>
> Accountant: "I will get right on it. I have been too busy recently."
>
> Auditor: "Why have you been too busy to do the reconciliations?" #2
>
> Accountant: "I have too much work to do, especially when I have to cover for a co-worker while she is on vacation."

Auditor: "Why do you have to cover for her while she is on vacation when you are already very busy?" #3

Accountant: "My manager told me to cover for her because there is nobody else to do it."

Auditor: "Why is there nobody else to do it? Why couldn't he bring in a temporary worker to cover for her?" #4

Accountant: "He told me that his manager wouldn't approve a temporary worker."

Auditor: "OK, I will talk to your manager. Thank you for your time."

Auditor to manager: "The accountant tells me that the reconciliations are late because she is too busy, especially when she has to cover for her co-worker while she is on vacation. She says you told her that you requested a temporary worker to cover the vacation, but it was not approved. Is that correct, and do you know why it was not approved?" #5

Manager: "That is correct. My manager wouldn't approve the request. He didn't tell me why, but I think he is worried about his budget."

Auditor: "OK, thanks. I will talk to her.

Auditor to senior manager: "I understand that the accountant's manager requested a temporary worker be hired to cover for a vacationing employee, but you denied the request. Is that correct and, if so, can you tell me why you didn't approve the request?" #6

Senior manager: "That is correct. I didn't approve the request because the accountant's manager couldn't explain why the coverage was needed, nor whether there was any risk if his request was not approved. He doesn't have a great record when it comes to managing his resources and budgets are tight, so I denied it."

Auditor: "Did you understand that without the additional resources, the reconciliations would not be prepared on time? If you had known, would you have approved the request?"

Senior manager: "I didn't know and if I had I would have talked to the manager. If we couldn't work out a way to smooth the workload so that the reconciliations would be completed on time, I would have hired a temporary worker. I will talk to him about the situation and how it should have been handled. This will be a learning experience for him and we will also have to figure out how to work with the available resources to catch up and ensure we don't fall behind again."

The root cause in this instance was the inability of the accountant's manager to express the business case for hiring a temporary worker combined with an inability to smooth the workload so that the reconciliations could be completed on time. When the senior manager was informed of the root cause, she was able to take actions not only to correct the current situation but to prevent a recurrence.

Chapter 11: Do we speak the same language?

George Bernard Shaw once said "England and America are two countries separated by the same language." I felt the same soon after I moved to the States.

While I was in Atlanta I learned to love the American way of life and people. Back then, England was class conscious. More to the point, Coopers in London seemed to give preference to those who were educated at the best schools, had multiple middle names (preferably hyphenated), and spoke with a certain upper crust accent. But in the States, I felt at home. Everybody was warm and welcoming. Nobody was cold and "snooty" (a particularly English demonstration of arrogance).

After I returned to London after U.S. exchange, I was promoted to senior manager responsible for technical computer auditing. However, my mentors (especially David Clark and James Fanshawe) felt, as did I, that being seen as a technician was not a viable path to partner. In addition, there were no Jewish partners in the UK firm (although plenty in the US).

My new love for America and my disaffection with my new position in London led to my decision that it was time to make a change. So I resigned from the UK firm and accepted an offer from the US firm.

When Stan offered me a position, he explained that he was concerned that the CAAG teams on the West Coast (in a typically American fashion, the US firm added an 'A' to CAG and called the activity the Computer Audit Assistance Group) had a poor work ethic. (Actually, he used an expression that was a little earthier, indicating he thought they were lazy S.O.B.'s.) He asked me to go to Los Angeles as the manager in charge of that office and shake them up.

So, I moved my possessions, including my TRS 80 II microcomputer, to Los Angeles and started working in a fairly large group there. George Hermann was the overall manager responsible for the group, which included San Diego, Irvine (between Los Angeles and San Diego), Phoenix, and Hawaii in addition to Los Angeles. They were not the slackers that

Stan portrayed. On the contrary, they were a dedicated collection of professionals (including people I still call friends, such as Rich Schmidt, another CAAG manager).

The language issue surfaced when I realized that my secretary didn't understand my English. Whenever I thanked her for something she had done for me, she had no idea what I was saying. It took me a month or more to realize, because each time I said "ta" she smiled, left my office, and never told me she didn't understand. "Ta" means "thank you" to English people, but means nothing to Americans. It was only when somebody mentioned that I didn't seem to appreciate her work that I realized what was happening. I asked her whether she understood that I was thanking her by saying "ta". She told me that she had no idea what I was saying, but it didn't really matter.

It mattered to me and I asked that she tell me whenever I said something she didn't understand. She was kind enough to tell me that she didn't understand half of what I was saying because I spoke too fast and softly, and sometimes pronounced words in ways she was not used to. As a result, I modified my speech and tried to use American pronunciations. After all, how can you be successful in business if people don't understand you? I believe it is my responsibility to make sure they do, rather than assuming they will take the extra effort to ask when they do not. To be honest though, I still speak softly (my expression) and mumble (what others say) and have to make an extra effort at times to be heard.

Years later, I had the privilege and pleasure of working with internal auditors in Singapore. Their English is so different from UK or American English that they call it "Singlish". For example, they will "on" or "off the light", where an American would say "turn on" or "turn off the light". This is easy to interpret, but I was confused for a while when they answered a question by saying that they would "revert" to me. In UK or American English, that means that they would change back into me – and of course, to the relief of many, there is only one of me! I guessed and was able to confirm that they meant that they would "get back to me".

∞

English is not the only language where one word has different meanings to people who ostensibly speak the same language. When I was with Home Savings of America as a Vice President of Internal Audit, I observed a three-way argument between a Thai lady (Nie), a Thai Chinese lady (Pat), an El Salvadoran male, and my secretary, who was Mexican.

Pat and Nie were scolding the El Salvadoran for talking to them inappropriately. His words and body language were offensive to them in their culture. He explained that he was only trying to help and he never used bad or offensive language when talking to ladies. At this point, the Mexican angrily told him that sometimes he used offensive language when he spoke to her. (I found out later that they had a 'relationship'.) He countered that he did not and demanded examples. She was happy to share a few, but he said that those phrases were innocent. She countered that in Mexican Spanish, they were offensive – even though they might not be in El Salvadorian Spanish.

I have learned not to assume that everybody uses and understands language, even the same words in the same language, the same way. It costs very little to simply ask for confirmation that what you hear is what they meant.

In more recent times, I have found that confusion over language, over different use of the same words or expressions in ostensibly the same language, continues and grows. Examples include:

- The word 'risk'. In common parlance, 'risk' refers to the potential adverse consequences or impact of events and situations. People talk about the risks of a car crash, earthquake, fires, financial losses, and so on. But for many risk practitioners, especially those who follow the global risk management standard, ISO 31000:2009, risk is "the effect of uncertainty on objectives". In other words, risk can have positive impacts. When talking to risk practitioners, I like to ask them whether they feel it is part of their responsibilities to help their organizations navigate both the adverse and positive effects of uncertainty, or just the negative. Only when I know we are talking the same language, and sharing a common understanding of key words, can we have a constructive conversation.

- The acronym 'GRC'. Most believe that it stands for 'Governance, Risk, and Compliance'. However, the Institute of Internal Auditors uses the acronym to refer to 'Governance, Risk, and [Internal] Control'. There is a huge difference. But the confusion is not just over what the 'C' stands for. People use the term 'GRC' without understanding what it means. When asked, they can say that it stands for 'Governance, Risk, and Compliance', but they can't explain what that phrase means. Some believe it is all about the management of risk, including compliance risk, and the oversight of risk management by the board. Others believe it is about the culture and ethical practices of the organization. I follow the concept of GRC advocated by the Open Compliance and Ethics Group (OCEG); it suggests that the long-term success of an organization is best achieved when all the pieces of the organization (particularly those responsible for governance activities such as setting strategy and objectives, making key operating decisions, monitoring performance, and providing oversight and executive direction) work together in a coordinated or orchestrated fashion, considering risk as they make decisions and staying in compliance at all times with both external laws and regulations and internal codes of conduct and practice. When people talk about 'GRC', I always ask them to explain what they mean. Otherwise, I find we are likely to be talking in what sounds like the same language but in fact we are not communicating at all.

If we are to have effective communications with others, we must take responsibility for what we say, what others hear and understand by our words, and what we hear and understand when others talk. This can be hard work, requiring skills (which need to be learned and then actively and consistently practiced) such as active listening and saying the same thing three times in different ways to ensure it is both heard and understood.

Unfortunately, most people are lazy communicators. They assume that people mean the same thing when they use particular words and expressions, but they often don't; they interpret what they hear using the dictionary of their own history and bias when the person they are listening to has a different history and bias; and, they don't confirm, through questions and repetition, that the person they are talking to has understood what they wanted them to hear.

Chapter 12: WIIFM

When Stanley Halper offered me a job in Los Angeles, he told me that he expected me to be a partner in the firm in a few years. I first had to obtain my CPA license (which I did in the first year). Then I had to obtain the support of the local general practice partners in the Los Angeles office and the other partners in CAAG. The process involved a nomination by CAAG, a vote in favor from the local office (Los Angeles), and then a confirming vote by the national office.

When I started thinking about the partner process, I assumed that it would be based on merit: the quality of the work performed, the revenue brought into the firm, and client satisfaction. How innocent and naïve I was, and what a life lesson I was about to receive!

I had made a number of friends among the general practice managers. (By general practice, I am referring to the managers responsible for the overall audit of our client's financial statements; they owned the client relationship and were specialists in financial auditing and reporting. Our role in CAAG was to support them with specialist work on computer-related financial reporting risks. The budget for computer audit work was granted at the discretion of the general practice managers and partners.) I had had been made welcome by them because I was a former financial auditor (with both a UK and US certification) and understood what they were doing, whereas almost all the CAAG members, from partner to junior associate, had a computer systems background. I spoke the same language and they trusted me.

I sat down with Don, a senior general practice manager who I knew was deep into the partner selection process. He told me that this was his second time to go through the process and his last chance to make partner.

Don mounted a considered, planned campaign. He made a list of all the partners and assessed his relationship with each of them. Where he assessed the relationship as weak, he developed an action plan to influence them in his favor. That might involve arranging lunches or other opportunities for them to get to know him better, finding ways to work on their favored projects or outside activities, and so on. He made sure to volunteer for task forces and special projects that might earn him recognition, and he told me without any indication of shame that he took as much credit as he could, even if he had little or nothing to do with the results.

Don told me that he was strongly supported by the managing partner of our office (let's call him Ben). Ben was disappointed that despite his personal campaigning with the Los Angeles partners the prior year, when it came to a vote to recommend Don for partner several partners had voted 'no'. As it was extremely difficult to progress without an unanimous partner vote, Don had not moved forward that year. Ben was adamant that Don should succeed this year, so he called the partners to a special meeting and told them that he needed everyone to support Don. They all agreed to do so. However, Don didn't want to take any chances so he continued to curry the partners' favor, especially those who had voted against him the prior year.

I left the meeting with Don shell-shocked. Is this what I wanted to do? Was it consistent with my personal ethics and values? I decided that I would need to campaign when my time came, which I expected to be in a couple of years. In the meantime, I would have to pay attention to my relationships with every partner and manager – the latter because they could influence the partners' thinking. But, I would not follow Don's example of stealing other people's credit. If I couldn't make partner based on merit, I doubted that I wanted to be a partner.

A month or so later, I checked in with Don to see how he was doing. He pulled me into his office, looking quite distraught, and closed the door. Apparently, the partners had voted unanimously to recommend him for partner, as expected. The next step was for the national office to send a very senior partner to interview him and several of the partners. Don told me that his interview went well, but when two of the local partners were interviewed they, in his view, "stabbed him in the back". Even though they had committed to support him, they had sabotaged his nomination by making negative comments to the visiting partner. He didn't know whether they had a problem with him or Ben, but either way his career at the firm was over and he would be leaving.

In Don's view, and I have no reason to believe him wrong, the partners had not acted with the best interests of the firm in mind. Don had the respect of every manager I knew, was considered the most proficient manager in the office, and had brought in significant new clients. But, the partners were political and vying for position and, through that, additional personal gain.

∞

At about the same time, I received another lesson in politics and personal gain.

Firm policy required that every year, for every client, the CAAG staff would perform a high-level review and assessment of the client's computer systems. It was called a 'classification review' because we would assess whether the systems were 'complex', 'simple', or somewhere in between; 'simple' meant that the financial audit team would be able to address all the financial reporting risks without computer audit specialist assistance. For example, there were no complex calculations that couldn't be audited manually. If the systems were classified as 'complex', that not only meant that the financial audit team could not address defined financial risks manually, but computer audit specialist assistance was mandated. This typically included some combination of technical assistance in documenting and assessing controls in the computer-reliant processes, the use of audit software (for example to reperform calculations), and the assessment and testing of integrity controls.

CAAG would complete and write a report documenting the classification review. The report would be sent not only to the general practice manager and partner, but to the CAAG group manager, the CAAG partner in charge of the region, and the CAAG partners in the national office (including Stan).

One day, I received an angry call from the regional CAAG partner, based in San Francisco. He said he wanted to hear why I had classified all the systems at a fairly large client as 'simple' and had not recommended any CAAG assistance on the audit. I explained that the reports provided a clear audit trail, that there were no complex calculations, and that the general practice audit team would be able to address all the financial reporting risks without our (CAAG) help. He asked if I understood that his personal performance, as well as that of the group manager, was based primarily on the number of hours of CAAG work. I confirmed that I understood, but prudently refrained from remarking that adding CAAG hours did not necessarily lead to savings in general practice hours. Sometimes, it just meant that total hours increased without an increase in audit fees – meaning that the overall rate per hour, a major performance metric, dropped and so did firm profits.

The regional partner could see he was not persuading me to change my classification assessment, so he tried another tack.

He asked if I was familiar with the firm's new audit software suites for general ledger and accounts receivable. I said I was very familiar with them. He then asked if the software suites would work with the client's systems. I said they would, but that they would not add value to the audit because existing client system reports provided similar information. In a voice showing his frustration with me, he asked about the relationship I had with the general practice manager and partner, and I replied that it was strong. He asked if they trusted me because like them I was a CPA, and I confirmed that I believed they did.

Then he went over the line. After asking whether if I had recommended audit software they would have accepted it, and hearing my answer that I thought they might, he paused. Clearly, he was thinking about ordering me to change my report and including a recommendation to use one or both audit software solutions. In the end, he told me was very disappointed in me. If I ever had an opportunity to influence an increase in CAAG hours I was to take it. He didn't care whether the audit needed or would benefit from the CAAG work, or whether it would have a positive (by reducing general practice work) or negative impact on rate per hour of overall engagement profits. He only cared about what it meant for him.

What's in it for me, or WIIFM.

∞

I had learned my first lesson about individual motivation, that while many (thank goodness) are driven by a desire to serve the organization, many are more interested in serving themselves.

Understanding what drives people is important for several reasons:

- As a manager, you need to motivate your staff
- You also need to influence others, your peers and your manager
- As an auditor, you need to understand why people act the way they do and how to influence them to accept your suggested changes
- It is also important for auditors to understand motivations when assessing fraud risk and investigating potential improprieties

I was faced with a decision: did I want to be a partner with a firm with this level of politics and actions driven by self-interest?

Over the next year, I worked with a variety of managers and partners. Most were hard-working individuals of character and integrity. However, there too many were focused more on WIIFM instead of what was best for their client and the firm. I decided to leave.

But there is an important postscript. Over the next few years, after I had moved on, I continued to stay in touch with many partners and managers at C&L. I saw the people who played politics and looked after their rather than the firm's interests prosper. For example, one individual who had little compunction about lying his way to the top was promoted to partner. However, it didn't take long for the firm's leaders to see through the politicians and with five years they had been fired.

I am told that the politics within PwC is far tamer today than it was in my experience.

Politics can get you to the top. It can even help you prosper at the top for a while. But over time it will create enemies and sews the seeds of failure.

Chapter 13: Where do I go from here?

When I decided to leave the firm, I was tempted to stay by Stan and the firm's managing partner. They flew me to New York and over dinner at a private club promised me their support in the partner process. But, although I hesitated for a month or so, I decided that the life of a partner was not for me.

After ten years with the firm, it was time to move on. Initially I agreed to join Disney Corporation as their computer audit manager. But while I was a big Disney fan, I was not a fan of their internal audit team. They were pleasant people but were not doing anything particularly interesting. I realized that I had accepted the position because it was somewhere to go after C&L, not because it was somewhere I *wanted* to go. It didn't excite me so I declined the job.

After talking to a few companies, I interviewed with Patrick Sheehan of Di Giorgio Corporation. Long since defunct, at the time Di Giorgio was a highly diversified company with revenues of about $2 billion and its headquarters in San Francisco. Its subsidiaries included an electronics wholesaler, a drug and related product wholesaler, a fruit juice manufacturer, a commuter airline, a tree farm, and a golf course and residential housing developer in Southern California; a grocery wholesale and distribution company on Long Island, New York; a plastics moulding company in the Mid-West; an automotive products company in Northern California; and, a wholesale and distribution company in the Netherlands.

There were a number of interesting challenges in the opportunity. I was going to be responsible for computer audit work across the organization, as well as all the financial and operational audits in Southern California. I would not be required to move but could stay in the Los Angeles area. I would be part of a small but very experienced team and we would be working on areas that the CAE, Patrick, had identified (through discussions with top management and the board) were significant risks to the organization. There would be variety and not the traditional audit approach of documenting, assessing, and testing the same key processes year after year.

Patrick was himself a draw. He was a charming, engaging, yet experienced auditor who was held in high regard and trust by the board and top management. I thought I could learn from him (and perhaps some of his charisma might rub off on me). Certainly, I felt and absorbed some of his passion for the company and was excited when given the opportunity to join the team.

The position was "senior auditor". This was a momentary issue, but Patrick explained that his title was "manager" and he couldn't offer me the same title. I reflected that "senior auditor" was better than "other", and that the job and opportunity were more important than any title. Certainly, the compensation and potential growth opportunity were excellent. I did not intend to stay in internal auditing, but to move into a management role after two or three years, either in Information Technology (IT), in Finance, or elsewhere. The beauty of Di Giorgio was that with many divisions in many industries, there should be many opportunities for such advancement.

In contrast to the Disney job, where I was running away from C&L, I was looking forward to and excited at the opportunity to work at Di Giorgio. As a mentor today, I give people the same advice: only take a job when you see yourself excited and running towards it. Don't take a job just to escape your current position.

Over the years, I have worked for a number of companies in a number of positions. As I look back, some were good moves and others were not so good. But, each time I was making the move towards what I believed was a good and exciting opportunity. I count myself lucky that most worked out well, some extremely well.

Chapter 14: Wearing a white hat

I enjoyed my time with Di Giorgio. Most of the amusing episodes related to work I did as the computer auditor.

The first was with the division in Southern California that manufactured orange and other juices under the brand name TreeSweet. Their CIO was a somewhat crusty gentleman and it took me some time before I obtained his confidence. I was visiting TreeSweet for an audit of their cash projection process (the CFO was consistently inaccurate with his forecast, which created a problem for the corporate Treasurer) when he asked to meet with me. He was concerned that one of his employees might target the company's systems. The employee was a senior programmer who had been with the company several years. However, the CIO had become suspicious, not because of any overt actions of direct comments, but because the employee was not acting in his normal way. He suspected that the individual was upset with his most recent performance review and salary increase, and that he might try to damage the systems in a way that would make the CIO look bad.

The CIO and I discussed what the programmer might do and how any inappropriate actions might be detected. I thought the CIO's plans were sound. While I offered my help, we agreed he could do what was needed without it.

Of course I stayed in touch and called the CIO every week or so to see what, if anything, he had found.

About a month later, he called me to tell me he had uncovered the programmer's plot. It was a truly devious scheme!

The programmer first sabotaged the weekly full and daily incremental backups. I should explain that the company made a full backup weekly and it was retained for four weeks. After four weeks, the oldest backup tape was re-used (this overwrote and therefore destroyed any data from the old backup). That way, there were always four weeks' data backed up (the latest weekly backup and three prior weeks) as well as the daily incremental backups since the last weekly backup. The programmer had inserted code into the backup routines so that the data was not backed up properly and the backup tapes were useless.

Then, he had inserted a "time bomb" that was designed to delete all data from the TreeSweet systems the day after the last viable backup was re-used (and destroyed in the process). In other words, the time bomb would explode when there was no way to recover the data from backup.

The CIO had been brilliant: he was able to see, through a review of system logs, that the programmer had accessed the programs that created the backups. He checked the code and found the logic the programmer had inserted – which he deleted. The CIO then reviewed the other program changes the programmer had made and found the time bomb in the middle of an authorized program change. Testing of the change by IT and users had not detected the bomb because it was time-driven.

The CIO informed me that the programmer had been fired and the incident was being investigated by the police.

Some auditors might have inserted themselves into the investigation. But, I could see that the CIO was quite capable of handling it by himself. With the approval of the CAE, I contented myself with monitoring his progress.

∞

The second incident was at the corporate data center in San Francisco. The company was using Hewlett Packard System 3000 computers for its corporate systems, including the corporate financial systems. These were excellent systems: reliable and easy to use. For a computer auditor who placed great value on the ability to perform data mining, their IMAGE database management system and Query software made writing audit software easy and fast.

I was doing an audit of IT general controls and met with the head of IT operations, Brian, to discuss some preliminary findings. I told him that the system had not been properly secured. Unfortunately, he did not believe me. Although he was responsible for the data center, including security, he was not a technical person and relied on representations from the Hewlett Packard representative that the password system was strong.

I thought I could prove him wrong, so I met with the corporate CIO, Marshall, and obtained his permission to do a little "white hat" hacking. We made a side bet of lunch and with nothing more than a standard employee signon I went to work.

Within a week, I was able to sit down with Brian and give him a printed list of all the employee user signons and passwords. I had won the bet. Without going into details, I was able to find a password for a low security area in a set of operating instructions. I used that to explore the system and found the file with all the passwords. It was protected from write but not from read access and was not encrypted.

I didn't use this exploit to make anybody look bad, or to trumpet my own capabilities. I used it to demonstrate to the IT folk that I had the ability to audit their systems, and to find ways in which to improve security and operating practices.

In other words, I used the exploit to make friends and influence people, not to make enemies. While there might have been some short-term benefit by writing a scathing audit report, I achieved longer term benefits in trust and the ability to effect change.

Some measure their value and effectiveness by the number and significance of their audit findings. I measure my value and effectiveness in terms of how management trusts and looks to me to help them be successful.

∞

On the topic of audit reports, Di Giorgio is where I had a memorable encounter with the CEO, Bob Di Giorgio. When it came to writing my first computer audit report, which I believe was on the topic of IT general controls over the corporate data center, I expected it to be an easy task. After all, if I could explain data base technology to CAG members, surely I could explain the state of system security to the board and top management. I was wrong. Patrick made me write draft after draft, each time simplifying the language and talking in terms of how the business might be affected by the issues I had identified.

A week after I issued the report, I was summoned to the office of the CEO. Bob Di Giorgio was the last in a line of Di Giorgio family members who had run the company, taking it public some years previously. He welcomed me warmly and said he had wanted to meet me. Bob blew away any concerns I might have had about meeting him by saying that over the years he had read many audit reports on the topic of computer systems and computer security. Mine was the first one he understood!

He commended me for taking a business rather than a technical perspective and we had a productive conversation about the company.

∞

A few months later, I visited the Dutch division, based in Antwerp, for an audit of their IT general controls. Initially, everybody was very friendly and open. But, when I found that the IT department consisted of just three people, the manager who ran operations and two programmers, and that nobody was reviewing or testing program changes made by either programmer, they cooled off. The manager said that he trusted his programmers and didn't see the need either for the other programmer to perform independent testing or for users to test program changes. He was supported by the division's general manager. I explained the risk: that while I had nothing but professional respect for the two programmers, people make mistakes. A mistake could lead to billing errors, failures to order the raw materials necessary for manufacturing, and so on.

Fortunately, one of the top executives was visiting and he asked me to join him in a meeting with the general manager. He asked about the audit and I told him what I had found. He expressed concern and asked the general manager what he was going to do. When the general manager tried to explain that his was a small company and he didn't agree that action was necessary, the executive became quite angry. Even though I was there, he told the general manager that he was taking a significant business risk. He used my own words, my own explanation of business risk, to justify his making this a high priority for the division.

Many years later, I would join my friend Jay Taylor, who leads IT auditing and more at General Motors, in asserting time after time that "there is no such thing as IT risk – only IT-related *business risk*." I was pleased to see the leading computer audit and security professional organization, ISACA, say essentially the same thing in its professional guidance: in both its guidance on IT-related risk management, and its overall COBIT framework.

Chapter 15: Awkward days

A few months after my meeting with Bob Di Giorgio, he retired and the company President, Peter Scott, took over as CEO. As good as Patrick's relationship had been with Bob Di Giorgio, it was weak when it came to working with Peter Scott. Patrick and Peter had clashed many times in the past and Patrick was not prepared to show Peter any particular deference now that he was CEO. Patrick relied on his relationship with the board and his well-deserved reputation for integrity and competence.

It didn't take long to the clash to come. Patrick took a firm and, in my opinion, unwise position on a relatively small issue. He raised what I would consider an opportunity for improvement, in other words, an internal control matter that was not particularly significant to the corporation's strategy or objectives. Management disagreed with the value of any change, so he took it to the new CEO – who also disagreed. Patrick decided to take it to the board, arguing that as the independent internal auditor it was his obligation to ask the board to decide when he and management disagreed. The board sided with their new CEO to nobody's surprise (even Patrick knew he would lose) and started looking for a new CAE.

We all went about our work, unaware that the board had decided that they needed a new CAE.

When I received an invitation to join the board for a dinner with the executive team, I was flattered. I asked Patrick about it and he said that from time to time the board would meet with highly-respected, up-and-coming managers to get to know them. I enjoyed the dinner and my conversations with the executives and directors until I was asked about my ambitions with the company. I told the director that I was looking forward to an opportunity to move into either a Finance or IT leadership role. The director asked if I had ambitions within internal audit, which made time slow down. I probably answered fairly quickly in real time, but my mind was buzzing with the question "why". Why was he asking about internal audit? Should I say I was interested in a CAE position, or just voice my respect for Patrick? My conscience shouted at me to be loyal to Patrick and do nothing to jeopardize his position. In the end, I shared that while a position as CAE might be in my future, Patrick was doing a fine job and I saw my next step as one into line management.

Less than a week after the dinner, Patrick came clean and told us he was leaving. He had been given a generous package and was moving to the next stage of his career. He shared with me privately that the directors and Peter Scott had been looking at me as a possible replacement, but after I had expressed a preference for moving into a line management position had decided to look outside the company. He had the grace to apologize for not letting me know before the dinner.

I was not particularly upset, as at that time I believed (correctly) that I needed to at least spend time in line management before leading an internal audit team. I was not sure whether my long-term future lay in internal audit, finance, IT, or operations. I was also reassured when I received a commitment from top management that when a new Director of Internal Audit started (Patrick had been promoted by Bob Di Giorgio), I would be promoted to Assistant Director of Internal Audit for IT and Southern California audits.

However, I was very disappointed when I met the new CAE. He had the credentials but not the experience to be an effective leader of internal audit. He accepted me as his deputy, but clearly was not happy. Suspicious at first, I think he was reassured when he heard I had not asked to be considered for appointment as Audit Director. But he still tested me. Fortunately, I had been hardened in the heat of the C&L political crucible, so I could see and easily handle his less-than-subtle maneuvering. While his financial accounting skills were greater than mine, my experience in public accounting was at least as solid as his, and I had built strong trusted relationships with top management across the organization.

The most troubling time was when Dawn, a new hire whom I had helped interview and recommended for the senior auditor job, was tasked with an audit at TreeSweet. In theory, as it is located in Southern California, this audit should have been performed under my supervision. But I was busy and had no objection when the CAE said he would supervise Dawn. After a couple of weeks, the CAE (who had stayed in San Francisco rather than coming down to supervise the new hire on site) called me. He said that he was worried about Dawn. She didn't call him very often and when he called It could be hours or even the next day before she called hIm back. The CAE asked me to drop in on Dawn at TreeSweet to see how she was doing, but not tell her in advance that I was coming. That way, and he made this very clear, if she was at the beach instead of at the office, we could find out.

I was disturbed by the lack of trust. I tried not to show it when I asked him to confirm that he wanted me to make a surprise visit to check up on Dawn. He said that was exactly what he wanted.

When you can't trust your own people, especially when there is no good reason for mistrust, they will neither trust you nor owe you loyalty. Everybody in the department knew what was happening, because the CAE was not private with his worries. Unfortunately for the CAE, everybody in the department felt his behavior was unjustified and unprofessional. In short order, they all left. The irony is that when I left, about a year after the CAE started, the only auditor left in the department was Dawn.

Chapter 16: A great but unlikely compliment

After a little more than two years, I felt it was time for me to move into a new position at Di Giorgio. Although my relationship with the CAE was still rather cool, he asked me to stay. But I told him it was time for me to move on. My plan was always to stay in internal audit for two years; if I was to grow my skills and abilities, I needed to move into a line management position.

I sat down with Pete Scott and told him that I was looking to move within the company. He was warm and courteous, thanking me for the work I had done and expressing support. He said that he would be very happy to see me as a Controller at any of his divisions or as his CIO. However, there were few positions that were at my level of seniority and compensation, and all but one had been filled within the last year or so. One position was open; he asked if I had any interest in moving to New York as Controller of the large wholesale company on Long Island, and I had to tell him that was one of the few areas where I would prefer not to relocate. Pete understood completely, being very much a West Coast man. He told me that while he would prefer to see me stay with Di Giorgio he would be happy to write me an excellent recommendation and serve as a reference.

After a short search, I joined Home Savings of America as a Vice President within the internal audit department, responsible for all IT audit activities and a variety of operational areas. I made it clear that I still wanted to move into line management after a couple of years in internal audit.

The CAE, Bob Broderick, had been promoted to that position fairly recently after a successful stint as the Vice President responsible for IT audit. Bob was an unusually humble man. While he had every reason to be proud of his successful career, he made a point of telling me that he thought I would be able to advance IT auditing beyond what he had put in place. He never put on airs, although he was not shy about making it clear who ran internal audit. He stood up for the department when the need arose, even though his official status would not meet today's criteria.

Although all of his direct reports (of which we were four) were Vice Presidents, Bob was not promoted to Senior Vice President for two years. Given that the common joke was that even the janitor was an Assistant Vice President, I don't think this was appropriate. Above Vice President were Senior Vice Presidents, First Vice Presidents, and Executive Vice Presidents before reaching the level of the President (Mario Antoci) and CEO (Robert Ahmanson) of the organization.

Furthermore, Bob reported to a Senior Vice President (SVP) within Finance. Even though this SVP reported directly to the President, Mario Antoci, there were more senior individuals within Finance and the CFO was an Executive Vice President.

Today's Standards for the Professional Practice of Internal Auditing (from the IIA) make it clear that the CAE must report administratively to a level of management that is very senior within the company, preferably to the CEO, and administratively to the Audit Committee to the Board. I don't believe Bob was sufficiently free of undue management influence over his activities as CAE.

I saw this in action in my only meeting with Mario Antoci while I was with Home Savings. One of the areas I was responsible for auditing was the Legal function. During the audit planning process, Bob told me that the SVP and President were concerned about the effectiveness of the Legal department because there was no General Counsel: each of the attorneys reported directly to the CEO. I agreed to perform an operational audit of the Legal function, with emphasis on whether the collective leadership was positively or negatively affecting their effectiveness and efficiency.

This was the first audit where I worked with attorneys. Each of the Home Savings lawyers was courteous, open, gracious, and helpful: an experience I have found consistently repeated over the years with few exceptions. They explained how they had divided responsibilities and each felt they did not need a General Counsel. None suggested that they should be considered for such a role either. However, they were not allocating work evenly, were not making good use of the outside law firms they turned to for additional expertise and resources, and it was clear to me that not only did they need consistent leadership but better systems for managing case status and workload. The business risk was that their valued insight and advice might not be available when executives needed (some executives were already bypassing them and going directly to outside counsel), and that some litigation may not receive the timely attention necessary for a successful resolution.

I crafted the audit report very carefully indeed. I wanted to make it very clear that each of the attorneys was not only capable but diligent and making a significant contribution to the organization. However, the risk to the business if the situation continued was significant: executives might continue to bypass the Legal team and obtain less than adequate advice and services, putting the company's strategies, plans, and objectives at risk. I made a number of recommendations for management consideration.

When I reviewed the draft with the attorneys, they were disappointed but recognized that the audit had identified facts (such as executives bypassing them) of which they were unaware. They agreed that action was necessary and they would support whatever the CEO decided was necessary.

My next meeting was with Bob and the SVP. The SVP asked a lot of questions and it was clear he very strongly supported the appointment of a General Counsel and was pleased with the business justification uncovered by the audit. Bob said that he would be meeting with Mario to discuss the audit, given the great interest in the topic he had expressed earlier in the year.

I was pleased to receive an invitation to join Bob when he met with Mario. I can still remember how stunned I was by the opulence (marble floors and golden tapestries) of the executive floor and the friendliness of Mario's executive assistant. Bob and I waited in her area until we were waived into the inner sanctum.

Bob and I were momentarily surprised to find that the SVP was already in the room and he and Mario had clearly been discussing my report, a copy of which was open on the table. However, Mario greeted us with none of the decorum that the surroundings seem to mandate. He showed himself to be very much down-to-earth and approachable, and soon demonstrated how good a listener he was.

Mario told me that he had read the audit report with great interest and wanted to hear more about the details. I opened my mouth to speak, but the only sound that could be heard was the SVP answering the question. While Bob and I just exchanged glances, the SVP laid out facts and business justification that not only were not in the report but on occasion were contradicted by the report. To give Mario credit, I suspect that he knew. However, he only had a few questions for me before saying he had the information he needed and that he would be meeting with the CEO to discuss the actions that would be taken.

Bob and I agreed that the correct result was probably being achieved, even though neither of us was happy with the SVP's intervention. Bob said he would talk to him.

Over the years, I have seen and heard of other inappropriate intervention, influence, and downright meddling by senior executives in the work of the internal audit function. I strongly support the IIA's position that the internal audit function should be owned by the Audit Committee[1] of the board (or equivalent governance body), that the CAE should report functionally to that committee, be appointed or dismissed only by that body, and have his or her compensation set by them. There will be more on this topic later.

For now, I want to talk about a great compliment I received.

---

[1] While I support the official IIA position, my personal preference is for the CAE to report directly to the lead independent director and attend not only meetings of the audit committee, but the governance, risk, and other committees responsible for the issues addressed by internal audit.

∞

Another area I was responsible for auditing, in addition to IT, was Human Resources. During the audit planning process, I met with the SVP for Human Resources.

Hazel Grandchamp was just like her name suggests: a grand, dominating presence. She must have been in her sixties, had been with Home Savings since its infancy, knew everybody that mattered, and was a force within the company.

I had hardly sat down in her office and explained my role within internal audit when she told me that I couldn't audit Human Resources (HR)! She was polite but firm.

I tried to explain that internal audit had a responsibility that extended to every function but she interrupted and said that she accepted our independent role. That wasn't the problem. We couldn't audit HR because we had never worked in HR and didn't understand the work they did. An audit of her area would be a waste of our and, especially, her time.

I told her that I agreed we were not experts in HR. However, I believed that as internal auditors we were experts in processes and internal controls[2]. I asked her to give us a chance to show her how we could add value to her operations. "Are there any processes you are concerned about? Are there any operational problems that you are having difficulty solving?" After a few moments' reflection, she said there was one problem and she would give us that chance I was asking for.

One of her departments was Salary Administration. Every position within the company was assigned to a grade level, and a range of compensation was established for each grade. The only variation was by state. For

---

[2] My good friend, Richard Chambers, uses the expression "you don't have to be a clown to audit the circus". While I agree with his intent, I prefer not to use this metaphor when I talk to management.

example, let's say the Vice President of Internal Audit position was assigned to grade 44. Salary for individuals within grade 44 was within a range from (hypothetically) $50,000 to $65,000 if the individual was in California. If the individual was in Arizona, the range would be adjusted to, say, $40,000 to $55,000 to reflect a lower cost of living.

The problem was that Home Savings was expanding rapidly, primarily through the acquisition of smaller organizations in states where we did not have a presence and therefore did not have established salary ranges. Salary Administration (SA) had to complete the necessary research and establish the salary ranges as soon as possible after the acquisition was completed (preferably before) to avoid operational and employee morale issues. But it was not. It was taking SA longer and longer to complete the work and the senior executives running the new operations were complaining louder and louder.

Hazel had been demanding that her direct report, the VP for Salary Administration (let's call him Jim) get on top of the problem. But all Jim would say was that he didn't have enough people to handle all the acquisitions. Hazel didn't accept this excuse, telling Jim that she had benchmarked his staffing to SA departments at other organizations. She had made adjustments for the size of Home Savings (it was the largest Savings and Loan in the US, comparable in asset size to a top twenty bank) and the number of acquisitions it was making. Her assessment was that Jim had 10%-20% <u>more</u> staff than at comparable institutions.

Hazel said that if we could help with this issue, she would be very grateful – although she made it very clear that she didn't think much of our chances!

One of my senior staff, Alan Marcum, had recently completed an IIA course on operational auditing so I asked him to perform the audit. I would provide guidance as necessary, but he would perform the fieldwork.

Alan met with the VP Salary Administration and then interviewed several of the staff. While the VP told Alan the same story as he had told Hazel, that he didn't have enough people and everybody was overloaded with work, Alan's observations were different. He saw that some people were leaving promptly at 5pm (the normal end of day) while others were working far longer hours. Some were fully up-to-date while others were far behind.

Alan and I discussed this and I suggested he gain an understanding of how work was assigned and progress monitored. We knew that each staff member was responsible for a geographical area, and I asked Alan to assess whether this meant that everybody had an equal workload, and whether they were able to make adjustments when a major project occurred, such as an acquisition.

Alan found that work was assigned purely based on geography, without consideration of existing workload. In fact, the VP did not monitor and had no ability to monitor actual workload. As work arrived it was passed straight to the appropriate desk without being centrally recorded. If the staff member at that desk did not have time to work on the task, it went into his desk drawer. When he was ready to start a new piece of work, he would take the oldest item from the desk drawer. The VP discouraged a busy staff member asking for assistance from anybody else, because he wanted to maintain expertise on each geographical area.

This did not totally explain the fact that some were working late while others had time on their hands. Diving a little deeper, Alan found that when special projects occurred (such as an assignment to assist in the implementation of new software), assignment to the special project was made regardless of current workload and work was not moved around to compensate for the new assignment. These special projects were frequent and the VP generally gave them the highest priority.

Alan developed a constructive set of recommendations to improve work assignment, monitoring, balancing, and so on. He led the closing meeting with the VP and Hazel. Hazel heard Alan with big eyes, frequently turning to the VP and asking him "is that correct?" He had to confirm Alan's description of the facts, and although he tried to defend his management of the department, Hazel was totally in accord with Alan's recommendations. She agreed they were the way forward.

After the meeting, Hazel called me. She told me that she had sent the CEO and Bob a letter commending Alan and me. We had surprised her and she would not only support our performing audits in HR, but be a champion for us across the company. She closed by inviting me to join her for lunch the next week, at which time I would have her permission to drive her Cadillac! The icing on the cake came at that lunch, when Hazel told me that I did not behave like a typical auditor. I had a business perspective.

Being singled out by Hazel as not being a typical auditor was meant and taken as high praise.

Chapter 17: When to suggest an answer

A couple of interesting things happened on the IT audit side as well.

Home Savings was always updating and improving its computer systems and a major part of our work involved participating in major systems projects to ensure sufficient controls and security were included. The IT department and all the major business users supported internal audit involvement.

One of my audit supervisors, an Assistant Vice President responsible for audits of the computer systems that supported the savings side of the business, was working on a major systems upgrade in the ATM banking area. At that time, I was lucky to have a solid set of direct reports that included Carla Williams (whom this story is about), Joe Throckmorton, Kathy Sanborn, and Bridget Timberlake.

Carla was an experienced IT auditor with excellent insight into the business side, having worked for a time in that area. To this day, I believe strongly in auditors who have line experience and therefore understand what it is like to run part of the business, especially when it includes responsibility for revenues and expenses.

Carla and I met to review the progress she had made. She explained that she had reviewed all the system deliverables to date, including the Requirements Definition, Systems Design, and draft User Procedures. Everything so far was looking good, but she was concerned that the project still had quite a long way to go and she had other projects that needed her attention.

We agreed that while it was desirable to continue to support this key project, our primary objective was to provide management with assurance that when it was implemented the controls over and security of the system and its data would be adequate.

Although the project team still had to complete development of the final product, test it, and turn it over to the users for their testing, the company's processes for testing and acceptance of the final product were excellent. Testing by IT and users was typically thorough, disciplined, and all we needed to do with regard to testing was to review the testing documentation once it was completed. The efficiency of the IT project was a minor element of our audit scope and given the other demands for Carla's attention, we should drop related audit procedures.

In other words, we should see if we could assess whether the *design* of the system, its controls and security, would satisfy our criteria. If so, we could issue a preliminary report indicating that if the system was implemented *as designed*, our opinion was that the controls and security would be adequate. We could update that report when we had reviewed the testing documentation and confirmed that the controls, as designed, had been sufficiently tested and found to be operating as intended.

Carla was comfortable with this approach and we moved on to whether we had sufficient information with which to assess the design of the controls and security.

Carla thought she needed additional information and was planning to meet with several users and IT developers. I suggested we use a "control matrix" to help us see where we stood. A control matrix is a simple table where each column represents a type of system transaction, such as a deposit or withdrawal, and the rows are where you assess whether the controls satisfy defined control criteria. We used control criteria that were based on what I had learned at C&L: completeness, accuracy, validity, and maintenance. So you take each transaction, in turn, and assess whether the controls adequately ensure that all transactions are completely entered, processed, and recorded. The controls that address that requirement are documented in the 'completeness' row for that transaction, as well as the assessment that they are adequate. Then you move to the next row, the next criteria, and identify and assess the related controls.

We were able to complete the entire control matrix, filling in the controls that satisfied each control attribute for every transaction. As we got towards the end, Carla started showing signs of discomfort. By the time the matrix was full, she was visibly concerned. She acknowledged that all control criteria were satisfied for all major transactions. She also confirmed that she was confident in her understanding of the controls. But, her experience was telling her that more work was needed.

We revisited the objectives of the audit, namely to provide assurance that the controls and security of the system, when it was implemented, would be adequate. She agreed that the control matrix had asked all the necessary questions and that the controls we had identified met the company's needs. She was able to put her prior experience aside and recognize that we had sufficient information to stop work until the testing had been completed.

This was an interesting exercise for both of us. Sometimes it is difficult to know when to stop work. There is always more to do, especially when your audit customers like seeing you at their meetings, etc. The control matrix helped us make the right decision and stop when there was no real value to continuing. I have used other techniques at times, such as sitting down at the end of the day (you could do it at the beginning, but I prefer the end) and making a list of the information you need before you can provide your considered, professional opinion on the adequacy of the controls (or management or risk.

∞

The second incident came while I was performing an operational audit of IT. Some of my interviews with the application development managers had identified a growing backlog of user requests. I was reflecting on this when I saw Dave Wagner, the Senior Vice President responsible for application development and to whom all those managers reported. He greeted me and asked how the audit was going. I told him that it was going well and that I was thinking about the user request backlog. I said that I was thinking about recommending a change in the way user requests were prioritized.

Dave looked at me over the top of his reading glasses and said "Norman, I don't think you should suggest answers until you understand the problem." That set me back on my heels and I left quickly, after thanking him for the comment.

I didn't know Dave that well at that time. I was lucky to get to know him much better in the years that followed, even working for him for a while. Dave had a sometime acid tongue, and I had just received a small dose of it – but the comment was not only appropriate and valuable, but gave me a telling lesson.

Too often I, as I have seen many auditors do often, have seen the *symptom* and suggested a cure without understanding the underlying problem. I discussed this earlier as the search for the root cause of a problem. In this case, I had leaped to the wrong conclusion. While the managers had told me about shared backlog problem, at his more senior level Dave had a far better appreciation of the issue, knew what could and should be done, and was actively working to address it.

In addition to talking to the people with tactical, "in the trenches", perspectives, I should have interviewed Dave and obtained his strategic view.

A similar mistake is made by talking only to managers and not talking to those who toil in the trenches. It requires a complete understanding before you can see the problem clearly, and only then can you suggest solutions.

In this particular case, when I did sit down with Dave he was able to fill in a major missing piece of the puzzle. He had discussed the backlog with each of the executives responsible for the user requests. Those executives had helped develop the current prioritization process. They were not concerned by the size or age of the backlog and, in fact, only a few items needed to be completed within a month or two. However, Dave wanted to do a little fine-tuning and we had a useful discussion about how that could be done. I added some value by being a sounding board for Dave's ideas and sharing my experience of how other companies managed the user request process.

Chapter 18: Learning about limits

After a couple of years, I was starting to think about my next move. While I had thoroughly enjoyed my time in the Home Savings internal audit department, when I was hired I had only committed to two years with the department; Bob knew that I was looking to move into a line management role.

I had gained the respect of one of the Senior Vice President responsible for data center operations, which included everything related to IT in the company except for the applications themselves.

Ron Reed was a dynamic and highly charismatic bundle of energy – with an incredible love for technology. His passion was his job and that was reflected in the number of hours he spent at work.

One of my favorite Ron Reed stories is when he and I were in his office having a discussion. Ron suddenly gestured towards the doorway; I turned and saw the head of the IBM representative (Bob Mugno) poking through it. Clearly, Bob wanted to say something and Rod signaled that he should go ahead.

Bob said that he wanted to show Ron the specifications for IBM's new disk drives and asked when Ron would have time to meet. Ron answered that he could meet at about 2. It was then about 11am so Bob appeared pleased and confirmed to Ron that he would stop by at 2pm. "No", said Ron. "2am". Bob laughed but Ron was serious: he had scheduled himself in meetings until 2am and meeting Bob then was, he felt, a good use of his time. Ron confided in me, after Bob left, that it also sent a message to IBM about who was the vendor and who was the customer.

Ron is not only a Type A personality and a workaholic, but one of the smartest people I have had the pleasure of working with – and I have worked with many who are genius level in their area. (Tom O'Malley, Jay Allen, Sir Brian Jenkins, and Stanley Halper come immediately to mind.) Later, he became a close friend, which he remains to this day.

Back to the story.

Ron asked me to meet with him to get my views on a reorganization he was planning of data center operations. He closed the door so we could have a confidential discussion then showed me a draft organization chart. Ron explained why he wanted to set up new departments and restructure his team. I told him I was flattered that he was sharing it with me and he said he wanted the opinion of somebody outside IT, plus I had an appreciation of the issues he was facing as a leader.

I saw a position on the organization chart for a Vice President, Administrative Support, with responsibility for information security, contingency planning, management of the IT facilities, accounting and procurement, standards, and more. That looked interesting so I explained to Ron that I was interested, if and when a position opened up where I could add value, in joining the IT management team. This seemed to both surprise and please Ron and he said he would give it some thought and discuss it with his manager, Warren Androus (the Executive Vice President responsible for all of IT and more).

We concluded our discussion without any promise on his part of a position, and with a commitment by me that I would let my manager know that I was interested in joining IT. I had the discussion with Bob Broderick the next week and he agreed, reluctantly but gracefully, to support a move should the opportunity arise.

I had to wait a while for that opportunity to arise and it came in the form of a call from Ron to meet. He offered me the position of Vice President, Administrative Support, reporting directly to him. But he had changed the position since he had shown me the draft organization chart.

In addition to what was shown on the earlier draft, the position now had responsibility for technical documentation (which was not a problem for me) and network design. Network design! I was shocked and said as much. While I had some technical IT capability, I had next to nothing in the telecommunications and networking area. I didn't want to take on responsibility for starting a network design function, including hiring the staff and not only setting myself up for failure but possibly causing some damage to the organization.

Ron told me that he was confident I would not only be able to handle the task but would do well. He was relying less on my prior experience and more on his assessment of my ability. He saw me as a thoughtful, analytical, and competent professional. Ron explained that he would help me as much as he could (he was an expert in this area, as in almost everything relating to technology), but he didn't think I would need much help. He was also hiring a Vice President, Telecommunications, who would be able to take over the network design area once I had it up and running well, in a year or so.

I decided to trust Ron. I was fairly confident I could handle the other areas and that meant that I would be able to allocate more time to this new area. In fact, I was lucky to inherit some excellent people (such as Joe Sileci, who ran facilities with authority; with his Sicilian name, he would occasionally threaten to call on his relatives to help him when he ran into opposition) and hire others (such as Ann Tritsch, who ran contingency planning; Sharon Smith, a brilliant technical writer who built a technical documentation team; George Szerbiak, who led the construction of two new data centers; and Jan-Jan Wu Gross and Dave Kovarik, who led information security and successfully implemented the ACF2 security system).

The year after I started, I had to complete performance appraisals for all my direct reports. They had all performed brilliantly and so I gave them high ratings.

Ron came to my office and told me that I would have to change the assessments. HR policy mandated that only a very small percentage of employees would get the top rating, the majority would be assessed as average, and a few below average.

I argued with him that this would not reflect their actual performance and he continued to respond that he had no choice but to follow corporate policy. But I won the day by asking Ron to name the top five performers in his entire area (and he had about 500 people reporting to him). Four of the five were on my team, and the others were in his top ten! He agreed to go back to HR and instead of making me assess my team on the required 'curve' he would assess all his 500 people, as a group, so mine could rise to the top.

Ron predicted that my analytical, logical approach to problem-solving would make me successful in starting the company's network design function. Without going into details, I can tell you he was right. I thought through the problem at hand, its objectives and the tasks that needed to be addressed as priorities, wrote a short paper that helped me crystallize my thoughts, and reviewed it with Ron and his other direct reports. That went very smoothly and I was probably more surprised than anybody else when the feedback was that I was heading in the right direction. I hired a young man to perform the detailed work, which he did very well, and when Ron hired a Telecommunications Vice President about eighteen months later I was able to hand off a solid program.

I learned two lessons from this experience: the first was that common sense (which is unfortunately not that common), allied with a logical and thoughtful approach, would help me accomplish tasks that I had never imagined I could.

After this, I refused to set myself limits – except where prior experience in the area was essential. I gained confidence in my ability to take on and conquer new challenges. This put me in good stead when I was asked to take on, for example, responsibility for the support of all Home Savings in-branch equipment and – much later – to start a risk management program.

The second came a few months later. The young man I had hired as my network design analyst came from a troubled background in South Central Los Angeles. He was a successful, diligent professional when he worked for me. But when the new Vice President, Telecommunications took over, his performance fell apart. He had problems at home, with his young family, and while I had been sympathetic and supportive, his new manager was a tough disciplinarian. Instead of responding to the pressure, the analyst disintegrated and started taking more and more personal tIme off at the expense of completing his assignments.

To this day, I believe that if he had stayed on my team, the young man would have worked his way through his personal crisis. I was not a great manager then (that story is in the next chapter) but I was a decent listener and knew when threats would not work.

∞

One of the toughest and saddest days of my life to that date came a little while later.

Ann Tritsch was my Assistant Vice President responsible for contingency planning. She had a very tough job, because the company had nothing in place other than backing up its data files on a regular basis. Not only that, but contingency planning was not a priority for the IT managers whose resources and support she needed. For the first year or so, Ann worked all hours and with both passion and dedication. She made excellent progress, which was recognized by IT management.

But then she started getting sick and having to take time off for recovery each time. Fortunately, her health condition was not serious and I knew she would catch up as soon as she got back to full health. However, the IT department had put in place attendance standards that were very strict and had punitive consequences when they were not met. My peers, especially in IT Operations, noticed that Ann had been out sick several times and put pressure on me to give her at least a performance warning.

I was very reluctant indeed to give one of my best employees any kind of performance warning. I am talking about a class lady that was not only excellent at her own job, but was always ready and willing to help her peers out as needed.

Then she got sick again and had to take a week to recover.

My peers took the issue to Ron and to the HR department. They asked how they could continue to enforce attendance requirements for their staff when I wouldn't do it for mine. It didn't matter that their staff were almost entirely hourly-paid employees while Ann was a highly-paid middle manager. I was instructed to formally counsel Ann.

I did what I had to do, went to my room, shut the door, and cried. Ann didn't take the counseling well: she became very angry, asking me whether this meant I didn't have confidence in her, whether I suspected she had not really been sick, and couldn't accept my words that we would get past this. Within a month or so, she resigned and left quickly. To this day, I don't believe she has forgiven me.

I didn't have any choice. But, it taught me the harsh lesson that many HR policies are good in the text books but awful when it comes to getting the most out of the workforce. As a CAE in later years, I would frequently argue with senior management (with occasional success) for HR policies that were designed to help management work with employees, creating a harmonious and constructive environment, rather than following the latest HR "fad".

Chapter 19: Empathy

One of the lessons that Patrick Sheehan hammered into me at Di Giorgio was that before I could be confident that I understood a problem and could make the appropriate recommendation for improvement (emphasized by Dave Wagner), I needed to understand what it was like "in the trenches", where the work was actually performed. Before I criticized others, I should understand and appreciate their daily challenges: the size of their workload; the pressures they felt from managers, customers, and peers; the difficulties presented by slow or inadequate systems; the cooperation they received from others on whom they depended; and so on.

It reminds me of the caution that you should walk a mile in someone's shoes before you criticize them.

As the external auditor, I rarely worried about whether somebody was already over-worked before reporting a controls issue that impacted the integrity of financial reporting. But as the internal auditor, I was more concerned with my ability to influence and effect change. In other words, letting people know there was a problem was not enough – there is no value in such a report unless action can and will be taken to address the issue.

Patrick told me that I needed to have more *empathy* for my internal audit customers. Empathy, understanding what it was like to walk in their shoes, would help me craft a report with recommendations that were practical, business-oriented, and achievable. Having empathy would help me influence and effect the change I desired and felt was necessary for the business.

He gave me a fold-out sign with the one word on it:

Empathy.

As he suggested, I kept it in a prominent position in my office. Every time I looked up, it reminded me that empathy was critical to my success.

I kept that sign in a prominent position from then on, and a photograph of my office twenty-five years later would probably have included it. (Also prominently displayed was a can I was given while I was at Home Savings, with its label carefully turned so all my visitors could see it: "Bullshit Repellent". When the need arose, I just reached for the can to send a message to my guest that I was more than a little skeptical of what he or she had just said.)

As I mentioned earlier, I think I was a decent manager and developer of people. But, I was definitely a driver with a clear focus and commitment to completing projects on time with quality. Missing a deadline or failing to deliver on a promised deliverable was not in my make-up. The job came first.

This was to change.

While I was moving along with my career, out of internal audit and into line management within IT, Home Savings was not doing as well with its goals. Bob Ahmanson retired as CEO but remained chairman of the board, and Dick Diehl stepped into his massive shoes as chief executive.

Home Savings was by far the largest savings and loan in the United States. It achieved this by focusing on individuals and families that had achieved a level of success and wealth. Its branches exuded the kind of atmosphere upper-middle class individuals expected, and its products were tailored to that clientele.

While it was able to retain its position as the market leader by concentrating on this profitable and loyal segment of the population, it was losing ground to Great Western and other savings and loans that had more streamlined operations and focused on a younger set of customers. For example, while young professionals might feel Home Savings branches were stuffy, Great Western branches were open and airy. In addition, Home Savings had stumbled with a couple of large acquisitions, including Bowery Savings Bank in New York.

The board and top management were concerned about the company's margins and operating costs. The board decided to make a change and brought in a new CEO from a mid-size bank. As might be expected, the new CEO brought in some of his own people, including a senior executive (John Ounjian) who had been responsible for IT at the bank. A political battle commenced; it was way above my head but was soon to impact my life in a massive way. Mario also left the company around this time.

In a reorganization of IT, Ron Reed was moved into a new position (he was seen as loyal to Mario) to make room for John Ounjian, and Warren Androus left. My role was changed (most of the activities seen as 'administrative' were consolidated under me) and I now reported to Dave Wagner. Dave had also lost some of his seniority within IT, and we all knew that this was not the end of the shake-out of IT.

The new CEO hired a consulting firm to help him drive costs down and efficiency up. The consultants went from department to department, each time making recommendations for change. They created what was seen as a rolling wave of downsizing. Managers knew that this wave would at some point reach their shores.

During this period, while IT was waiting, the CEO called a meeting of all Vice Presidents and above. He and his top lieutenants explained that our expenses were too high and we needed to make some significant changes. This was unpleasant but understandable news for us to hear and absorb.

What to this day I believe was unacceptable, although understandable in a way, was the presentation by the head of HR (Hazel had retired and been replaced by a much younger and assertive executive). He explained that this was an opportunity for each department head to make improvements in their team. While it was necessary to comply with all applicable laws and regulations (for example, not appearing to discriminate against protected classes such as females, people of color, or individuals fifty years of age or older) executives should take the opportunity to ensure that they were surrounded by people who supported them.

He made it clear, without saying so in so many words, that it was not only okay but was desirable to select those who would stay and those who would be laid off based on their loyalty to the manager, not their level of performance.

I believe this was morally and ethically unacceptable, even though it was legal and the company had every right to fire good employees in favor of friends.

As one whose performance assessments had always been exemplary, but whose mentors within the company had lost power and authority, I saw this as an indication that my job was at risk.

Sure enough, the wave reached the shores of IT. I was interviewed by the consultant. He asked many of the questions that I, in his shoes, would have asked. He even asked me for my opinion of where changes should be made to improve efficiency and effectiveness. But he didn't ask all the questions that would have enabled him to understand the value and set the right level of "administrative" services within IT, such as in contingency planning, technical documentation, and so on.

Within the month, I was given instructions to select employees within my department for layoff. While the numbers were somewhat (in my opinion) arbitrary, key positions in information security were not going to be affected and each of my areas would continue, if only with diminished numbers. The good news was that the selection for layoff would be based primarily on performance.

While nobody would come out and say it, it was very clear that I would lose my job. I had never met the new head of IT, John Ounjian, and he declined my request for a meeting. Clearly, I had the wrong friends in management and didn't have a place on his new team.

Although we now had a list of those who would be laid off, management waited months before they actually pulled the trigger. During that time, everything had to continue, projects had to be completed, and none of the individuals whose jobs were to end could be told. We were also forbidden to tell those who would be retained that their jobs were not at risk.

I changed, inside and out, from being a driver focused on achieving targets and meeting deadlines to being the morale officer for my people.

It wasn't only that I wanted to prevent people who were going to be retained from leaving.

It wasn't only that I wanted to keep people performing at a high level.

I wanted to make sure that everybody was acting in their own best interest. So, I dropped hints that stayed within the rules (barely) but would help people make the right decisions.

For example, I had hired a junior technical writer about a year earlier. She had been a secretary within IT for a long time but her ambition was as a technical writer. Unfortunately, she didn't have a lot of writing skills and her learning cycle was unacceptably long. As a result, she had been formally counseled and placed on a performance improvement plan. Tragically, her husband was a manager within IT that was also on a performance improvement plan. Both were destined to lose their jobs.

Neither was taking any action to look for new ones, and this disturbed me. I visited my lady quite often and tried to explain, bending but not breaking the rules, that she needed to act. I made it clear that individuals would be selected for layoff based on performance and that those who had been formally counseled were unlikely to be retained. But neither she nor her husband started looking for new jobs until after the axe fell.

Some have said that this experience, walking around the office as a morale officer, concerned more with the financial and emotional well-being of my people than of myself, made me human. It certainly made me a better, more empathetic manager.

I have learned that when people believe you care about them, are vested in their success, and listen and show respect for them as individuals as well as worked, they perform at markedly higher levels. They are loyal to you as you are loyal to them.

Something must have worked, because when I did leave the company and joined American Savings Bank, three individuals followed me.

Steve Costa was a consultant that had worked for me on special projects and I was able to hire to run one of my teams at American. Mary Beth Pastore was a former secretary of mine whom I had promoted into a senior accounting position at Home Savings; she did great things for me at American in the procurement and contract administration area, receiving high praise from our legal department.

The third was a lady whom I had not met before I interviewed her for an analyst position. When I asked why she wanted to join my team, she said that I had a reputation at Home Savings as a good manager to work for, one who listened to and cared for the success of every employee. Her experience at Home Savings had not been a positive one, and she was more interested in my qualities as a manager than in the company she was joining.

I believe that one of the best measures of a manager is in the number of individuals who follow him as he changes jobs. I have been blessed to have a number of great people on several of my teams over the years (including Katie Vo, Lorie Reynolds, Mary Beth Pastore, Steve Costa, Mike Wilmouth, and Marty Patton). Mike Wilmouth said:

> "Leaders come in many different forms and can typically be categorized as either dictatorial or humanistic. Professional and creative people thrive in an environment where guidance, not micro-management is provided to promote personal and professional growth and further creativity.

"I have known Norman Marks for many years and his leadership style is humanistic and genuinely cares about people no matter whether in his personal or professional relationships. As a result Norman has always been known to attract only the best of talent."

Chapter 20: The customer

Being laid off from Home Savings was not a great experience. Did it make me more human and a better manager? I think so. But it didn't do much for my self-esteem until I found out that rather than eliminate my position (as I was told during the exit process) IT management had split it. Two Vice Presidents were now required to manage the teams that I had been responsible for alone.

I was tempted to consult an attorney when I heard that the two individuals were people from the same ethnic group as John Ounjian, but I decided that it was healthier to move on.

Within a short time, Warren Androus offered me a Vice President position at American Savings (where he had moved and where Mario Antoci was the CEO) very similar to the one I had left at Home Savings.

American Savings Bank was a very interesting organization. It had been one of the culprits in the savings and loan crisis along with Lincoln Financial and a few others. It was acquired by the Bass family, who hired Mario Antoci as CEO, and it was widely assumed that at some point the Bass family would seek a buyer from among the larger savings and loans or banks. In the meantime, Mario Antoci had built a fine organization with several experienced executives from Home Savings and elsewhere.

Some years earlier, American had outsourced about 40% of its IT infrastructure and systems to FiServ, a large organization that specialized in outsourced IT processing for banks and other financial institutions. With Mario's blessing, Warren put together an 'all star' team designed to build a business case and then successfully bring back in-house the outsourced services. For example, the former CIO of Lincoln Savings was hired as project manager for the insourcing project and soon after I joined, Ron Reed came on as Warren's head of IT operations. My responsibilities included information security, contingency planning, all the accounting and procurement functions, standards and methodologies, special projects, and more.

Mario and his team were fully aware of the critical need to build loyalty and long-lasting relationships with American's customers. It was a much smaller institution than Home Savings and there was a great deal of competition, not only from other savings and loans but from banks.

With this in mind, all of us were told, and this was emphasized with training and awards, that should a customer call we were to drop everything to help him or her. It didn't matter whether it was a complaint or a general query, a matter for which we were responsible or something totally outside our area. If we picked up the phone and a customer was at the other end, we owned that issue until the customer was satisfied.

I received a call from a customer. She wanted information about how the company would handle her mortgage, something of which I was ignorant. But I was mindful of the company policy and took all her information and promised to call her back. It took several phone calls before I was able to find the right person for her to talk to. He said he would call the customer, so when I called the customer as promised I was able to let her know she should expect a call from this individual and gave her his contact information. That wasn't sufficient for me, so after a few days I called her again to ensure she had not only received the call but now had the information she needed.

This was an enriching experience. We have all suffered from poor customer service and as a result of this incident I know not only what good customer service is and how important it is to the organization's success, but how easy it can be if done right.

I have taken the lesson of this experience, that whoever receives the initial customer contact should own it until the customer is satisfied, to other companies where I have worked. It is a simple but powerful concept.

∞

Warren's plan to bring back the outsourced systems and infrastructure nearly worked. The project team was able to show that bringing it back in-house would cut costs by 30%-40% and potentially improve the quality of IT services to the business. But, the board told management to go back to FiServ and give them a chance to make a counter proposal.

We were astonished when FiServ came back with a proposal that they take over all but a few of the company's IT systems and infrastructure (in other words, we would move from 40% to 90% outsourcing) and this would cut total costs even deeper than the in-sourcing option. This was accepted and we prepared for layoffs. FiServ would need and make offers to very few of our people.

For some reason, which escapes me to this day, the CFO thought I was an asset that should be retained and offered me a position within Finance. However, that position was undefined and involved a move to Irvine – and a very long commute. I decided instead to look for another job. The company would surely be put up for sale, so any position was insecure, and the whole savings and loan industry was struggling to compete with the more efficient banks.

∞

I learned another lesson from my time with American Savings Bank. When Steve Costa set up his team, which included individuals to develop standards, life cycle methodologies, and tools for IT, everybody he hired was a 'mature' and experienced manager (such as the late Don Hayes, who led the development of an application life cycle methodology that was ahead of its time).

Even though positions on his team generally had only senior analyst titles, these grey-haired folk (if they still had hair) were interested in the challenges and opportunities to provide IT with leading edge methodologies and tools. They did a great job, in a limited period of time, and it is unfortunate that the FiServ outsourcing cut short the opportunity to see effect of all their work.

The lesson was that hiring motivated and experienced people may cost a little more per person, but they need little supervision or management, are far more productive, and in general create products that are practical, relevant, and useful to the business.

Chapter 21: The best job I ever had

The experts say that the best way to find a new job is through people you know, your network. When it was time to leave American Savings Bank, I contacted people in my network. Beate (pronounced 'Bea') Morrow, whom I had worked with at C&L when we were both senior managers, told me that Tosco Corporation was looking for somebody to lead their internal audit department. While I was not thrilled at the idea of going back into internal audit, Tosco had been one of my clients at C&L and I enjoyed the oil and gas industry. (One of my favorite clients while at C&L had been Atlantic Richfield, another oil and gas company).

I met Bill McDaniel, CFO of Tosco's larger division (Tosco Refining Company), and Jay Allen, the corporate CFO and hiring manager. The interviews went well, as did the interview with the chairman of the audit committee of the board.

I nearly lost the opportunity because I postponed my interview with the audit committee chairman twice, each time because I had time-critical projects to complete or meetings with senior executives. In the end, the chairman respected my professionalism and commitment to my employer and recommended me for hire.

∞

When Jay offered me the position as Director of Internal Audit, he told me that he was not hiring me for that job! He expected that after a few years, when I had rebuilt the department, I would move into a line management position. How wrong he would be! I was CAE for Tosco for more than ten years. Although I was offered one position after only a year (as head of procurement for Tosco Refining Company), and considered for another (CIO), top management and the board liked the work I was doing and wanted me to remain as CAE. They compensated me well and grew my responsibilities over time (for example, I added a contracts audit team to the internal audit activity, then an investigations unit, and even picked up IT quality assurance).

When I first became acquainted with the company, Tosco had grown from its beginnings as an investment vehicle in shale oil (Tosco stood for The Oil Shale Company) to own four U.S. refineries. The first time I visited its Bakersfield, California operation (which is where it had its IT operations), I flew there from Los Angeles in the company plane. But by the time that I joined the company, it had fallen on very hard times. It was leaking cash and struggling to remain afloat. Financial management met twice each day, just to confirm that they had sufficient cash to make it to the next meeting.

Tom O'Malley came to the rescue. Tom had made his fortune as a trader with one of the large Wall Street firms. With a small group of investors, he purchased a controlling interest in Tosco with a view to selling it off in pieces. Three smaller refineries were sold, leaving just the major asset, a refinery near San Francisco, California (Avon). But he couldn't find a buyer for the Avon refinery.

Tom decided to switch direction. He installed himself as CEO, one of his partners as President, and brought in additional heavyweight individuals to run the company. Jay Allen was hired as CFO and he, in turn, hired Bill Hantke as Corporate Controller and me as Director of Internal Audit. Tom also hired Wilkes McClave as General Counsel. Other key players included Jim Cleary, President of Tosco Refining Company; Bob Santo, Financial Reporting; and Pete Sutton, who led the teams that acquired crude oil for the refinery and sold its products, and the derivatives trading desk.

The company decided to diversify its operations and acquired a phosphate fertilizer company, Seminole, in Lakeland Florida. But within a few years, Seminole would be sold and Tosco refocused on its oil and gas refining business.

When Tom took over as CEO, the year I joined as CAE, Tosco was a $2 billion company and marginally profitable. By the time I left, more than ten years later when Tom engineered a sale to Phillips Petroleum, the company had grown to $28 billion in revenue and was the largest U.S. domestic refining company with eight refineries across the U.S.A.

It was a tremendous success. I attended the last call Tom and Jay had with the analysts that covered the company to review its quarterly earnings.

After Tom opened the meeting, one of the analysts interrupted and asked to speak. He said that he and the rest of the analysts wanted to show their appreciation for management's delivery of value to the company's shareholders over the last ten years. The analysts applauded, clapping their hands for a few minutes while those of us in management smiled at each other – somewhat in shock, because none of us had ever heard of analysts ever doing this.

Tosco was the best company I worked for, with the best management team by far. Tom was an entrepreneur and encouraged his management team to be entrepreneurial. Managers were empowered and respected. Those that performed well were rewarded, not only financially but through promotions.

The culture was excellent, with great attention paid to employee safety. (In later years, the Avon refinery had several fires and explosions and people lost their lives. Tom and the board decided that although this had been a highly profitable operation, it was also highly complex and difficult to operate at an acceptable level of reliability and safety, and they sold Avon.)

Although it was entrepreneurial and Tom was willing to take risks, risk-taking was always carefully thought through and only the best opportunities taken. These were the days before people were talking or thinking about enterprise risk management (ERM). But if they had, Tosco would not have had to make major changes in its decision-making processes to implement ERM.

Tosco grew primarily through acquisition. First, it acquired the Bayway refinery in New Jersey and related operations from Exxon. This doubled the size of the company, but did far more than double its value. Instead of a purely West Coast company, subject to swings in the relative prices of crude oil and refined products (gasoline, diesel, jet fuel, and so on) on the West Coast, it now had operations on both coasts of the U.S.A. Fluctuations in relative prices on one coast generally offset contrary swings on the other coast. This meant that there was more earnings stability, and that certainty was reflected by improvement in the company's share price.

In addition, the Bayway refinery was the only refinery directly on the New York Harbor. Without getting technical, this enabled the company to use the derivatives market to lock in ("hedge") the price of gasoline and jet fuel delivered to that market: a huge opportunity that Tom seized with both hands. He set up a trading operation, first in the corporate office in Stamford, Connecticut, and later at Bayway.

The Bayway acquisition included two other significant assets. It included a number of Exxon and other gas stations on the East Coast. Many years, earlier, Tosco had owned and operated gas stations but that had not been a success. Diversifying the business to include downstream operations such as gas stations was seen as adding value to the share price.

The other significant asset was the acquisition of some great management talent.

Dwight Wiggins joined the company from Exxon, where he had been the senior executive responsible for Bayway and other refining operations. He oversaw all our East Coast business. We also were able to persuade other talent from the Exxon Bayway team to join Tosco, including Tom Nimbley, the Bayway refinery manager. The new Bayway refinery team included some of the best talent I have had the privilege of working with over the years. In time, they would run all Tosco's refining operations.

Soon after, Tosco acquired a refinery and related operations in Ferndale, Washington. Tom was able to persuade an old friend, Bob Lavinia, to join Tosco and head up those operations. Bob had served (as had Tom) in the merchant marine and become a trader. However, he was able to adapt and become a strong leader and contributor to Tosco's success.

Other acquisitions included refineries in or near Philadelphia, St. Louis, Los Angeles, San Francisco, and New Orleans.

The company diversified again when it acquired the Circle K business in Tempe, Arizona (near Phoenix). It consolidated its convenience store and gas station business (together about 6,000 locations) in a new Tosco Marketing Company, in Tempe, led by Bob Lavinia.

At the time of its sale, Tosco was a $48 billion company; about 60% of its revenue and a larger share of earnings came from refining operations, the rest from its marketing company. Tom was CEO, Jay was President and CFO, and Dwight and Bob were Executive Vice Presidents and Presidents of our two divisions: Tosco Refining and Tosco Marketing.

∞

Top management and the board were extremely supportive of internal audit and gave me great freedom to be innovative as CAE.

I believe that for an internal audit function to attain world-class performance, and to be recognized as such by management and the board, it needs a combination of:

- An innovative CAE that has a deep understanding of the business, is able to influence and persuade management and the board as necessary to effect change, is flexible and able to adapt to changing internal and external business conditions, and is able to hire, retain, and motivate an outstanding team of professionals
- A talented team of internal audit staff that also has a deep understanding of the business. Between them, they have the technical skills and experience necessary to address all the risks that matter to the success of the organization (this may involve supplementing the staff using co-sourcing partners and guest

auditors from within the business), and the soft skills to listen, communicate, influence, and persuade
- The support of the audit committee, board, and top management. This includes providing the CAE with the necessary resources to address and contribute useful insights into the risks that matter to the success of the organization, and the freedom to be innovative and agile when needed

I had this trifecta at Tosco, and I believe I won the lottery in the process.

Chapter 22: Hiring the best

When I started at Tosco, one my first questions for Jay concerned my budget.

I was smarter than usual and instead of asking for a budget in dollars and cents, I asked him how many people I could hire. Although Tosco had an internal audit function before I joined, all of them had either left or were about to leave the company. (The internal audit department had been based in Santa Monica, near Los Angeles, and that office was being closed and departments located there moved to Concord, in Northern California. The one auditor that was still on staff when I joined decided to stay in Southern California and make a career change to be a personal shopper!) So, I had a blank slate – in many ways the best way to start a new position as CAE.

Jay told me I could hire three people (the same number as my predecessor had), and if and when I could justify hiring additional staff he would consider it.

Since he didn't limit me on budget, I decided to hire the three best people I could find, all with experience and talent. One would be an IT auditor and the others more financial and operationally focused. All three would be managers.

My first hires at Tosco were Lorie Reynolds, a fine IT auditor with a business orientation in addition to her technical skills. The other two were Laura (Morton) Nathlich and Michael Brooding. Laura was a charismatic, bright individual who I knew would go places. Michael, too, was bright; he was the more analytical of the two and rounded out the team well.

During my time in line management, I had learned to value intellect, curiosity, imagination, and the soft skills like communication over certifications and experience on a resume. Many of the best people I had on my teams in IT lacked the advanced degrees and professional certifications commonly held by internal auditors. In fact, I found that many internal auditors who claimed many years of experience in their resume really only have one or two years of experience – repeated multiple times. Not every smart person has the opportunity to attend the best schools or earn the right to put letters after their name (such as CPA, CIA, MBA, CISA, and so on).

One lady I remember was Deb, who worked with Dave Kovarik and Jan-Jan Wu Gross in the information security team at Home Savings. She and Dave were responsible for implementing the ACF2 security product, including placing restrictions on what the systems programmers could do without obtaining prior approval (such as changing programs or data to fix production problems when time was critical).

I was in the office that Dave and Deb shared when Dave told me that Deb had some news. She explained how she had been reviewing the ACF2 logs and noticed a strange change that had been made to the log file itself. She investigated and found that one of the system programmers (a group with incredible technical skills who sometimes thought of themselves as the gods of IT and above any security rules) had wanted to change a system file. But his access to that file was restricted. So, he found a way to alter the access rules to allow him to make the change, change the rules back when he was done, and then remove the log entries that recorded the fact that he had changed the rules. But, when he changed the log file, that change was itself recorded in the log file.

Deb didn't have the resume of a systems programmer, nor the advanced degrees that the rogue programmer held. But her curiosity, intelligence, and perseverance found the security breach and she was even able to identify the specific lines of code that had been changed, by whom, and when.

∞

I value those skills, attitude, and the potential they represent far more than any formal training or certifications. I had been working with an executive recruiter, the late Jamie Mahar, for some years. He always called me to tell me about his latest superb candidate. He extolled the individual for perhaps five minutes, during which time all he talked about were the candidate's certifications, formal education and training. I would shut him down by asking whether the individual could think.

Too many auditors are trained not to think. They are told to follow an audit program or checklist that somebody else created (in some cases, the checklist may have been developed some years earlier when the environment was different, and in other cases taken from a textbook without specific tailoring for the organization being audited). One of my tasks, as a manager and developer of these people, was to break those chains and insist that they think for themselves.

I had to find a way to assess each candidate's intellect, curiosity, imagination, and ability to learn during my interviews with them. The standard questioning based on the resume would not work, especially as candidates were generally prepared and trained by the executive recruiter on how to answer such questions.

When I interviewed with the chairman of the Tosco audit committee, Michael Tennenbaum, I learned a lesson in non-traditional interviewing. It didn't help that I had been told that this brilliant man was eccentric, driving a pink Rolls Royce Corniche to and from his aerie office near Beverly Hills (he was a Vice Chair with Bear, Stearns) and at the age of 74 skied a grand slalom course at Vail. I entered the meeting with the great man already a little intimidated, but I was somewhat prepared for the barrage of questions about why I had twice postponed my interview. He tested my 'mettle' and whether I could stand up to him and for myself. (This helped him assess whether I would be able to stand up to management should the need arise.)

I was not ready for the next line of questioning. Instead of asking about my prior experience, he asked me what I read. He explored how my mind worked, whether I was open to new ideas, could work with management and not just be a thorn in their side, and whether I had the intellectual ability to contribute as a direct report to the audit committee and an advisor to top management.

When I interviewed potential new hires, I wanted to obtain the same kind of insights into their mind – brilliant or stale. So, I developed a style of interviewing that many find unusual. It has multiple benefits: in addition to helping assess people's ability to think, it gets past the barriers created when recruiters train their candidates how to answer questions during an interview because I ask questions they cannot predict.

The essence of the interviewing technique is to help the candidate first become comfortable by asking them questions about their resume and why they have applied. They are ready for this and confident in their replies.

Then, I describe a situation (based on a real life experience that they should understand, at least in principle) and ask how they would approach an audit. If they ask for an audit program, that would conclude the interview. But, if they ask questions to improve their understanding of the underlying risks they would earn points of respect.

It doesn't matter whether they come up with the same approach that I would take, or even if they overlook an important issue. What matters to me is whether they are able to think through a situation they have never encountered and suggest an audit approach that makes sense and demonstrates that they have an intellect and can use it.

I have been told that candidates are not able to read whether I am satisfied with their answers and whether they are doing well in the interview. But they do say that I make them feel comfortable and stretch their ability to think 'on the fly'. That is what I am trying to achieve and it seems to have worked well over the years.

In hindsight, I have been blessed to have had the support of some brilliant people over the years. I am very proud of the teams I have led. Of course I have made mistakes and some of the hires didn't work out as well as I had hoped. But, most of the mistakes occurred when I made the mistake of placing too much trust in an individual's resume and too little on their intelligence, or placed too much trust in a direct report to hire well without ensuring that they understand how to assess intellect, curiosity, and imagination.

∞

I mentioned before that one way to assess a manager is to see how many people follow him as he or she changes jobs. I have been lucky to have quite a few do that as I moved to a new company.

Another measure is how well your people advance in their careers. I am proud of the number who have moved into CAE, CFO, and other senior positions. I thank them for making me successful through their hard work.

At Tosco, I started the internal audit department by hiring only managers. That is an approach that I continued as I built the department at Tosco (to as many as 28 in the internal audit part of my team by the time the company was acquired) and hired internal auditors at my subsequent companies.

∞

My style of auditing is very much focused on addressing the risks that matter and working collaboratively with management to improve the way they are managed.

This requires individuals who can leverage their experience and intellect to drive business-practical change, rather than individuals who can only follow an audit program or checklist.

Risk-based auditing is not about selecting a sample of transactions and testing whether they meet certain conditions, then reporting on whether the controls are working as desired. It is about assessing whether the risks that matter to the success of the organization are being managed at acceptable levels. While some level of transaction testing is usually involved, interpreting what you see as an auditor and finding ways to improve business operations is far more important.

It is true that you can probably hire three senior auditors for the price of two audit managers, or a larger number of people if you hire junior staff. However, not only do junior staff have less to contribute than managers in terms of ideas – and the ability to influence management – but they also require supervision and training by managers.

It is my experience that the time required for an audit manager to supervise a senior auditor, including helping them with defining the project scope and approach, reviewing the work during and after the audit, and rewriting the audit report, is at least as much time as they would require to perform the audit themselves.

At Tosco, we built and maintained an internal audit department that performed more audits at a lower total cost than our peers (based on benchmarking directly with them as well as using IIA benchmarking studies), and was respected by the board and management for making a significant contribution to the organization's success.

Management knew that when we performed an audit, they were going to work with dedicated, experienced professionals who had the ability and desire to help them be successful. You can do that when you are staffed with managers. It is far more difficult when you have a less experienced team.

∞

The Bayway refinery in Linden, New Jersey, frequently entertained visiting dignitaries. I was in the refinery one time when the Refining Company Controller (Steve) called me over. He told me that the previous week, he had been with Dwight Wiggins when the Governor of the State of New Jersey visited and took a tour of the refinery.

Steve told that that as part of his description of the business, Dwight told the Governor that internal audit "gave Tosco a competitive advantage"! Why was this possible? The internal audit team gave Dwight assurance and therefore confidence that his processes and controls were managing risks to the operation, and our contracts audit team was helping drive costs down and quality up.

That same year, I was in Phoenix for a Tosco Marketing Company executive team meeting (I attending both the Refining and Marketing companies' executive meetings when I was in town) when Bob Lavinia introduced a guest: the Republican candidate for Attorney General of the State of Arizona.

Bob went around the table, explaining what each of his team members did. "This is our CFO, he makes sure we are financially sound...... Here is our head of Marketing, who leads our advertising and branding programs...." He continued in this vein and then he saw me, hesitated, and then said "This is Norman Marks, who runs our internal audit team. He makes sure we stay efficient."

You can look in the mirror and tell yourself you are good looking. But the only praise that matters is from somebody you respect, or your customer.

Chapter 23: Humility and respect

My first office at Tosco was about the size, perhaps smaller, than an average walk-in closet. It took me a while before I was able to figure out where I could put my desk, computer, and chair so I could both sit comfortably to work and talk to somebody who came in to chat.

Right outside my office was a coffee room. In fact, you entered my office from the coffee room.

One day, I went to make myself a hot drink and a tall gentleman was at the coffee machine. He smiled, wished me a good morning, and asked my name. I told him and said that I was new to the company and the Director of Internal Audit. I pointed to my office and said I would like to chat with him at some point to learn more about the business. I asked his name, which he told me was Jim Cleary. When I inquired where he worked, he said he worked in the office of the President.

Later, I was talking to Bill McDaniel and he told me that there was only one person in the "office of the President". Jim Cleary was the President of Tosco Refining Company (Tosco's primary division; Dwight was to have that title later).

The humility that Jim showed in this chance meeting was not an act. It was an attribute of the man, Jim Cleary.

Before he was promoted to President by Tom O'Malley, Jim had run the Avon refinery. Although disputes between the union members and refinery management were unfortunately common, Jim always acted as a gentleman (although he had a temper and you didn't want to be the target when he was angry) and respected every employee. It is not too strong to say that the union workforce had similar respect for him and that helped the company navigate disputes when they arose.

Dwight shared the same attitude with every manager and worker, and was rewarded with respect in return.

Both men trusted their employees to work diligently and professionally. But when anybody acted in a way that jeopardized safety or reliability, they were quick to take action.

The media make it sound as if management of oil and gas companies, and of refineries in particular, are more concerned with profits and the share price than they are with the safety of employees. I can't speak for other companies, but my experience at Tosco (and at each and every one of its refineries) is contrary to that perception.

Safety was always the first item on every single refinery team meeting, including the meetings of the executive team. Every incident was investigated thoroughly and tough questions were asked of those involved in both incident and near-misses (where there could have been an incident, but we were lucky). Direct supervisors and their managers were called in to explain what happened, why, and what action they were taking to ensure it didn't happen again.

My office, like most of the executives, was inside the refinery. We were personally at risk should there be a fire, explosion, or chemical release. To portray our executives as less than fully committed to the safety of our employees, our neighbors and the community, and the environment in which we live, would be unfounded and contrary to the facts.

I was and continue to be proud to have been associated with the management team at Tosco, who always put people ahead of profits.

I am also proud to have worked with people like Jim Cleary, Dwight Wiggins, Tom Nimbley, Tom O'Malley, and many more at Tosco who acted like gentlemen. They didn't talk about 'empowering employees'; they just did it, listening to them, learning from them, and always showing respect.

I have tried to demonstrate the same qualities as a manager. I have great respect for the people on my team. I know that they often have greater insights and better ideas than I. They see things from a different perspective, which can be very valuable. So I listen and learn from them as much as I can.

I know not only that I can only be successful if I have a strong team (my success is only a reflection of their success), but that when they feel respected, empowered, and appreciated their level of work increases.

∞

In Phoenix, we had many internal candidates for positions on our internal audit and contracts audit teams. They came from all parts of the business and I was surprised, as internal audit is generally seen as a path into the business rather than the other way around.

Although I had direct reports for each of my areas, where possible I liked to be involved in the hiring process. I interviewed one young individual who worked in Finance and wanted to join internal audit. When I asked why, her answer was "Internal audit is the only department in the company that seems to be having fun! Every time we pass your offices, we see smiles and hear laughter." She heard the sounds of happy, empowered and respected employees who knew they were making a difference.

On another occasion, I was leaving my Phoenix office at about 7pm when I saw one of my managers, Loretta Forti-Corson, still busy at work. I stepped into her office and was welcomed with a smile. I asked Loretta why she was still working, to which she replied that she would be leaving soon but had a few things she wanted to finish first. I knew she was married and asked if her husband would be making dinner. She laughed "no". I said something about him being very patient as he waited for his evening meal. She sat back and said "Norman, I am having too much fun to leave right now."

Chapter 24: The risk-based internal audit plan

Tosco was the first time I had to develop an audit plan of my own. At Di Giorgio and Home Savings, I had responsibility for a part of the organization and so I was a contributor to the plan. But I had never created one of my own.

At that time, around 1990, leading internal audit practitioners (like David McNamee) taught an approach that I followed initially. It involved building a list of all the organization's processes, facilities, business units, and so on. This was called the "audit universe". Then, each item in the audit universe was 'risk-ranked' by assessing a number of risk factors such as:

- Time since the last audit of the area
- The significance of any control weaknesses identified by the last audit
- The materiality of the area (assets, revenue, and so on)
- Whether any new systems had been implemented since the last audit
- Whether there had been change in management
- Significant changes in the business
- The complexity of the business model, accounting, systems, and processes
- Issues identified by other assurance providers (including external audit)
- Concerns raised by management

The typical risk assessment model (generally created in Excel or similar) had a dozen or more of these risk factors, often weighted to give more emphasis to some factors than others.

The result of this risk assessment model told the CAE which areas to include in the current year's audit plan.

But the risk-based approach generally stopped there, with the audit team performing a "full scope" audit of each area included in the audit plan.

Some internal audit functions performed a second level risk assessment. This identified the higher risks within the area and these became the scope of the audit.

This two-step approach was typically called "risk-based auditing".

I tried this out in the first year, a year in which I was very much in a learning mode when it came to understanding the business.

But I quickly started tinkering with the model. I wasn't happy with the idea of a full-scope audit, where we would look at the entire business process or unit and assess the adequacy of its controls. It simply used too many of my scarce resources (auditors). As an economist by schooling (at the London School of Economics) I understood the concept of 'opportunity cost': the cost of doing one thing was not simply the out-of-pocket cost of the resources employed; it was also the lost opportunity of doing something else. When we spent time looking at low-risk areas in, for example, accounts payable, the cost was the lost opportunity to spend that time looking at higher risk areas in accounts receivable.

Some organizations today perform a second risk assessment once they have prioritized their audit universe. They take each higher priority area and identify the highest areas of risk within that unit or process, and that is where they focus their audit of that area. The result is an audit plan where the area is determined by relative ranking of risk factors and the scope of each audit is based on a risk assessment of the risks within that area. In other words, the unit, process, or location to audit is the result of risk-ranking the audit universe. But what is audited in each selected unit, process, or location is based on the risks within that unit, process, or location.

But I felt then and now that this leaves internal audit assessing risks and related controls that matter to the local business but not necessarily to the enterprise as a whole.

I took a different approach. Instead of populating my audit universe with business units, processes, locations, and so on, I went one level down and included the risks within each of the above. I then compared these risks across the enterprise and ranked them against each other.

The ranking would be based on their significance to Tosco, not just to the location. For example, I might identify "payments to consultants" as a high risk area within procurement and accounts payable. That would be compared to the "accuracy of customer pricing" within billing and receivables to determine which audit was the greater priority and should be included in the audit plan.

I considered this a risk-based audit planning process that resulted in addressing the more significant risks to the organization. The engagements in the audit plan were "focused audits" – focused on those areas within each process or unit that represented the greater risk when viewed with a wider lens, the lens of the entire organization.

∞

During this time, I attended a number of conferences and answered a number of surveys where the question was asked: "How large is your audit universe?" The intent was to compare the number of auditors to the potential number of audits. Most people answered with the number of business units, locations, and processes – what they considered "auditable entities".

I had fun with my answer. Since I could audit any process or area many different ways, I answered that my audit universe was infinite. (If asked to explain, I might take the example of accounts payable and say that I could perform a controls audit; an operational efficiency audit; a search for duplicate payments; a search for indicators of fraud; an audit of controls over payments to contractors, sole-source vendors, and so on; an audit of controls over payments to vendors in China or Mexico; and so on, and so on.

∞

One of the byproducts of the revised audit approach was that I was able to cut the average audit from several hundred hours to (typically) less than two hundred; many were only 120 hours or less.

With a small staff (just four auditors in 1992, including me), we were able to complete about 50 audit engagements. A better to way to think about that is that we were able to assess the controls over more than hundred risks (if the average audit addressed a couple of risks).

On average, my audit teams completed about 12 audits per person each year.

But this still wasn't enough for me. While it was "risk-based", we were still thinking about units, locations, and processes. We were not stepping back and thinking about the risks that matter to the success of the enterprise as a whole.

A jaw-dropping moment happened when I explained my risk assessment and audit plan to the audit committee of the board.

The CEO, Tom O'Malley, sat in on audit committee meetings in the early years. While this was sometimes intimidating, I was pleased to see him give the audit committee and internal audit his valuable time and attention. (He was always 100% present. In other companies, I have seen the CEO flit in and out of the meeting, sometimes taking committee members away to have private discussions – and disrupting the committee in the process).

Tom made a lasting impact when he asked whether I had considered risks related to the blending of gasoline, diesel, and jet fuel. As it happened, I had — but it was not considered high risk; it was more a compliance issue than anything else. I told Mr. O'Malley that I would revisit the risk assessment and he agreed that I should. (This was a subtle hint that I heard and understood!)

When I talked to Dwight Wiggins after the meeting, he told me that when he was with Exxon they performed an enterprise-wide risk assessment. Jet fuel blending was identified as their #1 risk! Poorly-blended jet fuel could lead to Boeing 747s dropping out of the sky into densely-packed urban areas, with the potential to bankrupt the largest (at that time) company in the world. A few years later, I saw the effect of poor blending of diesel fuel when Southern California drivers had major "dieseling" and "pinging" problems and fingers were pointed at us as well as a few other oil companies.

So, I moved to an approach where I identified the top risks to the achievement of the company's objectives (a *risk* universe instead of an *audit* universe), and then identified the engagements I could perform to provide assurance that the controls were adequate with respect to those risks and advice where they did not.

This, for me, is modern risk-based auditing.

I use a metaphor to explain how this is different.

In the old days, I might decide to perform an audit of my car. After all, it is a high-risk area. So, I will assess the quality and condition of the engine, steering, tires, air conditioning, etc. Perhaps I will find some defects and recommend service and repairs.

These days, I would consider my objective: traveling from my home in San Jose to the airport in San Francisco (42 miles). The risks include a breakdown of the car, an accident involving my car or others, traffic congestion, and weather. My audit would include looking at aspects of the car that I rely on to address these risks, including not only the condition of the engine and so on, but whether I am tuned in to traffic and weather on the radio. I would also consider how I can ensure I am sufficiently awake (if my flight is at 6am) and how I would know whether to take an alternate route.

The older audit is focused on auditing the car; the second is auditing my ability to arrive safely and on time.

∞

Initially, I would sit down with the executives and discuss their business plan and objectives. That was a good start but many business objectives (such as maintain a positive cash flow) are never actually stated. So I needed another tool.

I attended a presentation where another CAE showed us how he discussed enterprise risks with the management team (remember, back in those days nobody was talking about enterprise risk management; risk managers were typically responsible for insurance). I liked the graphic he used and have updated it as a discussion tool for every company I worked at since.

Figure 1 (below) shows the 2010 version.

Depending on the executive and how he or she liked to work, we might look at every entry on the diagram and I would ask him to identify those that were significant within the context of the organization's strategies, goals, and objectives. Then we would look to see if there are any risks that were not on the chart and talk about whether they were significant.

But the purpose was not just to rate the chart entries. It was to stimulate a wide-ranging discussion of the state of the enterprise.

The end result was satisfying in a couple of ways. First, the broad-based discussion of the business was very well received by the executive. I frequently heard that ours was a rare opportunity for the executive to think broadly about the business, rather than focusing narrowly on his area and worries. This contributed to our mutual respect and understanding: a valuable asset that I was able to leverage whenever it was necessary to talk about the condition of risks and controls in his area. Secondly, we had a shared understanding of the risks that mattered. I was able to use that to build the risk-based audit plan.

Figure 1: Risk Universe Discussion Tool

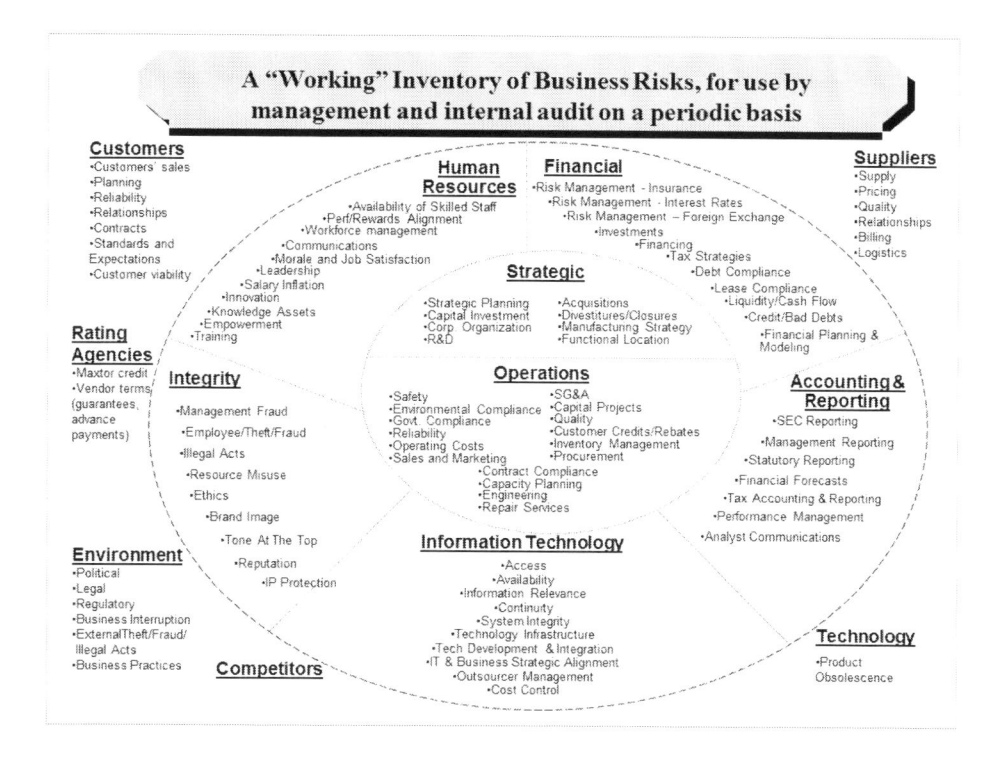

A "Working" Inventory of Business Risks, for use by management and internal audit on a periodic basis

Customers
- Customers' sales
- Planning
- Reliability
- Relationships
- Contracts
- Standards and Expectations
- Customer viability

Rating Agencies
- Maxtor credit
- Vendor terms (guarantees, advance payments)

Integrity
- Management Fraud
- Employee/Theft/Fraud
- Illegal Acts
- Resource Misuse
- Ethics
- Brand Image
- Tone At The Top
- Reputation
- IP Protection

Environment
- Political
- Legal
- Regulatory
- Business Interruption
- External Theft/Fraud/Illegal Acts
- Business Practices

Competitors

Human Resources
- Availability of Skilled Staff
- Perf/Rewards Alignment
- Workforce management
- Communications
- Morale and Job Satisfaction
- Leadership
- Salary Inflation
- Innovation
- Knowledge Assets
- Empowerment
- Training

Strategic
- Strategic Planning
- Capital Investment
- Corp. Organization
- R&D
- Acquisitions
- Divestitures/Closures
- Manufacturing Strategy
- Functional Location

Operations
- Safety
- Environmental Compliance
- Govt. Compliance
- Reliability
- Operating Costs
- Sales and Marketing
- SG&A
- Capital Projects
- Quality
- Customer Credits/Rebates
- Inventory Management
- Procurement
- Contract Compliance
- Capacity Planning
- Engineering
- Repair Services

Information Technology
- Access
- Availability
- Information Relevance
- Continuity
- System Integrity
- Technology Infrastructure
- Tech Development & Integration
- IT & Business Strategic Alignment
- Outsourcer Management
- Cost Control

Financial
- Risk Management - Insurance
- Risk Management - Interest Rates
- Risk Management – Foreign Exchange
- Investments
- Financing
- Tax Strategies
- Debt Compliance
- Lease Compliance
- Liquidity/Cash Flow
- Credit/Bad Debts
- Financial Planning & Modeling

Suppliers
- Supply
- Pricing
- Quality
- Relationships
- Billing
- Logistics

Accounting & Reporting
- SEC Reporting
- Management Reporting
- Statutory Reporting
- Financial Forecasts
- Tax Accounting & Reporting
- Performance Management
- Analyst Communications

Technology
- Product Obsolescence

∞

I developed a "rolling" audit plan that had two elements: a fairly solid plan for the next quarter, and a list of prioritized projects that I hoped to be able to initiate later in the year. Even the next quarter's plan was subject to change, should the business and its risks change.

I told management and the audit committee that the purpose of the rolling audit plan was to be agile. It was not only able to adapt to include audit engagements around new risks and remove engagements where the risk had diminished, but I was now able to respond to requests for assistance from management or the audit committee. Other internal audit departments allocated up to 40% of their audit plan for management requests, but I felt my approach was better.

Each quarter, or more frequently if needed, I would include a review of the audit plan in my report to the audit committee. I would discuss what had been completed, what I expected to do in the next quarter and by year-end, and explain why projects (and risks) had been added or removed from the audit plan.

The audit committee and management readily endorsed this approach, as it demonstrated agility and the flexibility to adapt and change as the business changed – and the business was certainly changing. It was growing fast, primarily through acquisition but also organically as Tom's strategies were paying off and our market share (and profits) expanded.

Tosco went from revenues of $2 billion in 1990 to more than $28 billion in 2000. My internal audit staff also expanded during that time, from 4 to 29 (including me). In other words, the internal audit staff grew at about half the pace that revenues grew. However, neither I nor the audit committee believed that we were leaving significant risks on the table.

The risk-based approach enabled me to run not only an effective internal audit department, but one that was highly efficient. When I looked at internal audit cost benchmarks (such as the GAIN study from the Institute of Internal Auditors), we always came in significantly below the average cost per dollar of revenue.

Chapter 25: My first frauds

Over the years, I have performed or managed more investigations than I can easily count. It's a responsibility for which I can take professional pride, but always with at least a touch of sadness that people commit these acts.

Sadness that sometimes is lightened by humor!

The first fraud I heard about was while I was an audit senior at Coopers in London. One of the senior partners, Chris Lowe if memory serves me well, told a group of us that he had just returned from a trip to the States.

Apparently, a year earlier one of the firm's U.S. clients had asked their local audit partner to lead an investigation into a suspected fraud by one of their top sales executives. For a reason that was never explained to his satisfaction, the U.S. firm decided not to do the work themselves and asked Chris to come over and perform the investigation. Chris completed the assignment and reported to the executive management team that the sales executive had indeed diverted a substantial sum of money to his own account.

The trip Chris had just completed was to attend a dinner hosted by the client. As Chris entered the room with the client's CFO at his side, he saw the sales executive in the middle of a group of company personnel – clearly enjoying himself with a glass of champagne in his hand.

Chris turned to the CFO and asked, in a typically British fashion, whether the company had accepted his report that the sales executive had been stealing. "Oh yes," the CFO replied. "But without him we would have no sales."

The company had decided not to discipline let alone fire the executive. Perhaps, some speculated, the U.S. firm had suspected that the "tone at the top" of this company was not as ethical as you should expect from a public company and that was why they had not performed the investigation themselves. If they had, and the client had decided not to take action, the U.S. partner might have been required to report this to the S.E.C. – and the firm would lose the client and its fees. Since the investigation was not performed by the U.S. firm but by an affiliate organization (the U.K. firm), reporting to the S.E.C. was not required.

Chris left it to us, without saying a word on the matter, to decide for ourselves who was less ethical: the sales executive for stealing, the company for not firing him, or the U.S. partner for steering clear of the investigation.

∞

I didn't run into any more frauds (only attempts by an employee to place a logic bomb to create havoc – see Chapter 14) until I joined Tosco, when two unusual situations came up in my first few years.

In the first, one of the audit team was performing an audit of safety at the Avon refinery when she found a discrepancy in the safety reports. These were regular reports to management by the refinery safety department of the number of accidents that resulted in injuries, the number of lost days, and the number of near-misses (incidents that could have, but didn't, lead to an injury). She was able to determine that the analyst in the safety department had deliberately manipulated the statistics to make the safety record look better than it was. The analyst admitted that she had done this. Her motive was not financial gain; she was hiding her manager's poor performance.

We all commit so-called "white lies", for example when our spouse asks if her new dress makes her look fat! The analyst thought this was an innocent white lie. But the potential harm was huge! Refinery management was not aware of the decline in its safety performance and therefore had not taken any action to investigate its causes and take necessary corrective actions.

In this case, appropriate disciplinary action was taken against both the analyst and her manager. Although there was no proof of complicity in the fraud by the manager, he signed the report and should have known it was fraudulent.

The second situation, a couple of years later, taught me more about human moral weaknesses.

Donna Philpott, the Assistant Controller for our refining operations, called me. She had just received a call from the California Bar Association telling her that one of our employees had filed a curious complaint against one of their members.

The employee, who was an accountant in our Concord office, alleged in his complaint that he had entered into an arrangement where the attorney would set up a dummy corporation and send Tosco invoices for fictional services. Our employee would arrange for the corporation to be set up as a vendor and for the invoices to be paid. (He had approval authority for invoices under a certain value.) The agreement was that the attorney would split the proceeds with the employee.

The complaint was that the attorney had kept all the money to himself! Clearly, he couldn't be trusted!

We investigated and found a couple of other vendors with the same postal address as the one in the complaint. One of those vendors was managed, not in the Concord office, but in the Seattle office. We didn't have access to the complete history of transactions in that vendor's accounts, so I called the Seattle Controller, Tim.

My team and I had, I thought, been very careful to keep the investigation quiet. I am a strong believer in limiting the number of people "in the know" to ensure that the potential culprit doesn't hear about the investigation until we are ready. The first risk we are managing is that he might destroy evidence. In addition, sometimes other people are involved, potentially including individuals in management. We don't want them to know, for the same reason.

Finally, and this is important, we must be careful not to damage anybody's career or reputation by letting others know their conduct is being investigated. In many cases, the people we suspect of inappropriate conduct are innocent; if people (especially in management) have heard they were suspected of fraud that might lead their managers to have questions about their performance and lose trust in them.

So, when I called Tim to ask for his help on a confidential matter and told him we needed the history on a particular vendor, his reply shocked me:

"But Norman, I was expecting you to ask for information on three accounts, not just this one". Someone in the Concord Controller's office had loose lips! After I hung up with Tim, my next stop was to talk to Bill and Donna and stress the importance of keeping this kind of information to themselves. The next time I was in Seattle, I had a similar conversation with Tim, because the investigation was common knowledge in that office.

The individual involved eventually confessed to fraud and the last I heard, he was a former employee in police custody.

∞

I formed a set of principles from these experiences that have served me well over the years, although at times they have been difficult to observe:

1. Anybody, even your closest 'friend' is capable of committing fraud. Circumstances change and anybody can, in a moment of weakness, rationalize theft and fraud.
2. It is critical to keep investigations confidential. There is a great risk to morale, let alone people's reputation and careers, when investigations are public.
3. Never assume guilt. For a start, that is a legal definition and judgment that should only be made by the company's attorney. But, even more importantly, we don't have all the facts to make

that determination until everybody has had a chance to tell their story – and that includes the individual suspected of the fraud. Often, I have had to hold my investigators back from their growing suspicions because the 'target' has not had a chance to respond; when they did, they sometimes had proof of innocence.

There will be more on the topic of fraud and investigations in later chapters.

Chapter 26: Not all auditors hate risk

The Treasurer at Tosco was a senior member of the Finance team, highly respected by company leadership. He had been a key member of the management team during the lean years at Tosco; shortly before I joined when the company was "leaking cash", he had led twice-daily meetings of the financial team to ensure there was sufficient cash to make it to the next day!

So it was important that we make a good impression when we performed our first audit of his area.

At the same time, he was a gruff curmudgeon (he reminded me of the late, great Alastair Sim as Scrooge in "A Christmas Carol") that scowled every time I saw him – and other executives told me that he shared that disposition with everybody except the CFO.

So, I set the auditor, Laura Morton (now Nathlich), two tasks: the first was to perform an audit and provide an objective assessment of whether the Treasury function was meeting the needs of the corporation; the second was to get the Treasurer (Craig Deasy) to smile!

Laura exceeded my expectations (something she went on to do regularly).

As I had expected, Craig's area was in very good shape. It reflected his personality as a disciplined, careful individual that had a deep understanding of the business and its needs.

But, Laura identified one issue that only deepened Craig's frown.

She pointed out that the company's investment policy limited overnight investment of cash to the safest of all investments, which had the lowest of all rates of return. While this was the policy that had been approved by the board, the level of risk being taken (clearly a very conservative one) was inconsistent with the general attitude of the company to taking risk!

The company was a significant "player" in the commodity derivatives market, not only to hedge the price it would pay for its raw materials (crude oil) and the price it would obtain for its refined products (gasoline, diesel, jet fuel, and so on), but it also had a truly speculative position. (The manager in charge of our derivatives trading desk was permitted to make speculative trades of several million dollars, subject to supervision by Pete Sutton, a Vice President. Over the years, he was consistently profitable.)

So it was taking millions of dollars of risk in the commodities market but unwilling to take any risk in its overnight investments?

Laura recommended that the investment policy be reconsidered. That was a wise move. Only management can decide how much risk it is willing to take, but we (as the independent and objective internal audit team) can challenge them when appropriate.

Craig reluctantly agreed that Laura had a point – not on technical controls philosophy but on business grounds. He discussed it with the CFO and they agreed to change the policy.

I met with Craig and Laura to review the final report before it went to the audit committee. He gave Laura a reluctant smile and acknowledged that it was a professional audit.

Since then, when I talk to groups of internal auditors about 'world-class internal auditing' and 'how internal audit can add value', I ask "Do your audit customers smile?"

But the other lesson for me was that internal auditors should not try to eliminate every risk they see.

In my early years, we would identify "findings" and assess the level of risk they presented. The level of risk (high, medium, or low was the typical scale) would drive the sense of urgency when we reported the issues and recommended corrective action by management.

This audit was one of the first where I applied the lessons I had learned in line management, that it is not about eliminating risk – it is about taking the right risk, based on understanding the potential downside, the potential upside, and the cost of any actions.

When auditors come to me with an issue (what we used to call a "finding", but no longer because of the accusatory nature of the word), I will often ask them: "What would you do if you owned the company? Is this something you would change or would you accept the risk on business grounds?"

I had a second situation of this sort a year or two – one that shocked both the audit committee and the CEO!

∞

Lorie Reynolds and I performed an audit of information security over the company's primary data center in Concord, California. By now, Tosco had grown significantly, adding a second large refinery in Linden, New Jersey (the Bayway Refinery, acquired from Exxon) and a smaller refinery and gas station business in Ferndale, Washington (acquired from BP). But, the company's financial system and other legacy applications were run at the Tosco Refining Company (TRC) data center and managed by TRC's IT department, led by S. Denny Smith.

We knew going into the audit that the legacy systems were quite old, written in COBOL, and severely patched over the years. They were no longer supported by the vendor, but generally met the requirements of the users.

(As an amusing aside, initially the IT folk gave me the respect technical people often give accountants when it comes to technical matters – little or none. So, as part of an audit of the refinery's legacy system – one of those COBOL applications – I decided to read the code and was able to point out a number of coding errors. (Rather than delete superseded code, they had 'branched' around it because they didn't fully understand the purpose of the code. There were two failures here: first, when they wrote or maintained code, they didn't document (whether in system documentation or in Notes within the code) what they were doing; second, when they branched around code rather than deleting it, they created a risk that a future change would activate the original code and cause the program to fail.) By pointing out how they had made these errors, and demonstrating that I could not only read but critique their work, I obtained their lasting respect.)

What we didn't know until we performed the audit was that the only security over the legacy applications was within the applications themselves – and that only applied to online transactions. There was no security to speak of over batch jobs that accessed the application files for overnight and other processing.

The risk was high. While we believed that user controls would prevent any major failure when it came to either financial reporting or other critical business processes, the risk of business disruption from a security breach was significant.

But we didn't make the leap to insisting on immediate corrective action. For a start, we knew that the company planned at some stage to move much of its IT production to a new data center at Bayway. We didn't know when that would happen or what would move.

Lorie and I met with Denny and his manager, Bill McDaniel. We learned that management planned to shut down the entire Concord data center in favor of a new Bayway data center. In addition, because of anticipated company growth and a desire to upgrade to a modern set of applications, the plan was to replace the legacy systems as part of the data center move.

Lorie and Denny continued their conversations, considering what options were available to enhance security over the legacy applications. Unfortunately, they agreed that the cost would be high. When compared to the level of business risks posed by the security deficiencies, and considering that the legacy systems would be replaced, they were both reluctant to recommend that management make a significant capital investment in new security products.

When I presented the results of the audit to the audit committee, with the CEO and CFO in attendance, I told them that this was an area of high risk – but that I was not recommending that they take any action, except to continue to monitor management's migration to the new data center and applications. (These days, now that we have a risk management language, I would say that "I agree with management that this is a risk that should be accepted".)

My words were met with astonishment. They had never seen a CAE fail to recommend action on a high risk area!

But, I stood my ground. If I owned Tosco, I would not make the capital investment necessary to upgrade security.

Taking a business perspective is essential to world-class internal auditing.

Internal auditors should understand that business is not about avoiding or limiting risk, it is about taking the right risk. I have learned that all internal auditors should consider themselves business people who have a job as internal auditors. Their work should be intended to contribute to organization success, not just point out deficiencies or "findings".

Where it is appropriate to accept a risk or even to take more risk (because the risk is acceptable or even desirable if the organization is to succeed), auditors should not be afraid of standing tall and saying so.

Chapter 27: Loretta and Wow! audit projects

Loretta was in the middle of one of my non-traditional audits and I can understand why she said she was having so much fun she was reluctant to go home.

One of the great influencers on my professional life has been Tom Peters, the business speaker, writer (co-author of *In Search of Excellence* and many others), and one-time McKinsey consultant. I attended a presentation he made on the topic of "Wow!" Without going into everything he had to say, every radical thought and message he shared, there was one moment that has affected every audit I or my people have performed ever since.

Tom told a story about an individual who was charged with updating the company's corporate safety manual. This had every sign of being a very boring project, so she set out to find a way to make it interesting and vital.

She changed the project objective from being a simple update to making the manual a product that was truly relevant and useful to managers and staff – as Tom explained it, she set out to make the project "a thoroughgoing review of how safety and environmental issues contribute to making this a GPTW/Great Place To Work" (Tom loves his acronyms!). No longer would it be something that sat on a manager's shelf gathering dust – there only because the company made him put it there. It would help create an environment that would attract and then retain the best employees.

Tom Peters makes his presentations freely available on his web site (www.tompeters.com), so I can share some quotes with permission. These come from speeches he made at the begging of the technology revolution that led to embracing the Internet, the rise of Apple, and more.

"We are in the most profound revolution in over 500 years and this revolution places over 90 percent of the white-collar worker jobs in jeopardy over the next decade….The 10 percent who survive will make it

137

because they have reinvented their work to be full of passion, excitement, emotion, and dreams (and a few noble fiascoes here and there)."

Tom talked about making every project a "Wow!" project. He explains it as something you would want to tell your grandchildren about. A Wow! project:

> "….is dynamic, stimulating, a major bond builder among co-workers, a source of buzz among customers, and inspiring, exhausting, hot, cool, sexy, where everyone wants to be."

When we did our audit planning, my Tosco Marketing Internal Audit Director (Rick Klaus) and his team had identified capital spending and the Authorization for Expenditure (AFE) process as a relatively high risk area that should be audited. His justification was the very high level of capital spending by the Marketing Company, especially compared to the level of profits, and the need to ensure capital was focused on projects that would drive revenue and/or lower costs.

Rick and Loretta (who would be the audit project lead) came to me with a proposed scope and objectives. The plan was to review the process for reviewing AFEs that had been submitted by the field to Finance (where they were handled by a team led by Mike Passaretti, a graduate of my internal audit team at the Bayway refinery). The audit focus would be on how Finance confirmed authorizations, recalculated and verified the business justification, obtained all required management approvals, and after the project was completed performed a post-implementation review to validate that spending and benefits were as described in the AFE.

This was a very traditional audit approach and I probably demonstrated how I felt about it by yawning (purely for effect).

I am great believer that internal auditors need to get out into the field and listen to managers and staff in the trenches if they are to understand the business, its risks and opportunities.

Tom Peters talked about this:

> "If you want to understand how a business really works, talk to the janitor".

Now I am not going to say that I spoke to the janitor, but I did spend a lot of time talking to the people running the business. At the Refining Company, I talked to refinery unit operators, line managers, procurement people, pipeline operators, oil tank managers, and so on. At the Marketing Company, I similarly talked to the people who ran the company from the front lines and interacted with its customers and suppliers every day.

I not only met with convenience store managers, but spent time riding with district managers as they drove around their areas. That gave me the opportunity to get to know them, their troubles and concerns, as well as see them in action as they worked with individual store managers and staff.

On one of those excursions, the district manager told me about how one of his store managers had come up with a great idea. His combined Circle K store and Union 76 gasoline station was at one corner of a major intersection in Los Angeles, with two of the other corners occupied by other branded gasoline stations. The city had sent a notice to the manager letting him know they would be performing major street upgrades at the intersection that would close much of it (including access to all three gas stations) for several weeks. The district manager helped him put together an AFE requesting a modest investment in a new entrance to our unit. The benefit would be huge, as ours would then be the only open gas station at this very busy intersection.

The AFE was approved, but it took the division's headquarters people a couple of months to review and approve the spending. By then, the roadwork had been completed, the intersection re-opened, and the opportunity lost.

Both the district and other managers of our store operations believed that the delay in this AFE was typical. In fact, they told me that there was a greater risk to the business from such delays or even failing to approve AFEs than any risk that might be created from capital projects that were not justified.

I shared my experience with Rick and Loretta and we changed the objective for the audit.

Instead of the traditional definition of scope and objectives, I asked them to answer this question:

> "Does the AFE process meet the needs of the business, considering the risk of inappropriate expenditure, the need for timely decisions, and the administrative cost of the process?"

Loretta found the traditional part of the audit, assessing the controls over the 'risk of inappropriate expenditure', easy and straight-forward.

But the challenge when it came to timeliness was greater – and more interesting.

It was relatively easy to find out how the process worked. Once a month, the division CFO gathered all the Vice Presidents and they collectively reviewed all the AFEs and the analysis prepared by Mike Passaretti and his team. They would take about half a day to discuss them and decide which they would propose should move forward and what the priority was for each.

The next meeting, typically the following day, was with the division CEO, Bob. The CFO and all the Vice Presidents would review with Bob the AFEs they believed should go forward. When he felt that the total was too high or disagreed with the VPs' recommendations, the executives had to debate which would be approved, which might be deferred, and which would be declined. This meeting also took a half-day on average.

Because of the intense review and approval process, each executive was careful to ensure all the AFEs they proposed had complete and accurate analyses included in the package. Mike and his team were equally careful with their review and analysis. This all took time.

It was clear to Loretta, as it was to all the Vice Presidents and the CFO, that the process was too long, consumed far too much executive time, and often cost more than the spending itself (if you count the cost of the VPs' time)!

The question was why the process was this way.

The CFO and VPs all agreed, usually with language they wouldn't use with children around, that they hated both the all-VP meeting and the meeting with Bob. They said they didn't have the time to spare and asked for our help to get the process – both time and cost – under control.

Loretta and I met to talk about what we were to do. Rather than share my opinion, for once I did the smart thing and asked Loretta for her opinion.

At first, she didn't know what to say. But as she realized she could say what was on her mind, and with some gentle guidance from me, she said it: the CEO was the problem. He was the only one who wanted these long and expensive meetings. Only when he was persuaded to change his mind could it be changed.

I knew Bob quite well, having worked with him before he moved into his current position with the company. He was one of the executives with whom I met frequently to discuss the business and he had shared a number of confidences with me.

I was sure that he would listen to Loretta and had a suspicion he would find it easier to understand himself if he met one-on-one with her. Both a formal meeting with the CFO present and a larger meeting with the three of us (Bob, Loretta, and I) might make it harder for him to look in the mirror.

And so it was. I persuaded him to meet with Loretta and she, in turn, trusted me when I told her she would not only be safe but would enjoy herself.

I admit that I was a little nervous as I waited in my office for Loretta. Then she appeared in the doorway, all smiles!

She told me that the meeting went brilliantly. Bob was charming, as usual, and showed great respect for her – even though she was 'only' a manager. He let her explain what she had found and that the long process was preventing timely investment to seize market opportunities. In addition, not only was it consuming a lot of expensive executive time, but it was taking them away from running the business.

This was critical, explaining the issue in terms of how it affected the business and its success. Auditors who talk in their language (what I call "technobabble"), rather than the language of the executives they are attempting to inform or persuade (which is the objective of an audit report) are unlikely to succeed.

Loretta said that Bob responded with silence, clearly thinking about what she had said.

Then he shocked her by telling her that he was the problem. He recognized that his insistence on discussing and approving every AFE could not continue. Bob told Loretta she had done an excellent job and that he would like to talk to me.

When I met Bob later that week, he repeated his praise for Loretta. Then he asked for my opinion. Again I was smart and didn't give him my opinion straight away. Instead, I asked him why he wanted to approve every AFE.

After a short hesitation, he said that perhaps he should only approve major capital expenditures instead of every one. I concurred, saying that was what I was used to and would advise.

But I kept at it. Why had he insisted on approving every AFE? This was not what he had done in his previous positions with the company, nor was it what he was used to working directly for Tom O'Malley – a consistent and effective delegator.

Then he looked again in the mirror and saw his true self.

"Norman, I can see now that I didn't trust my direct reports enough to make these decisions!"

We talked about this for a while. Either he had the wrong people in these key positions, in which case he needed to replace them, or he needed to trust the people he had and delegate more effectively. He didn't hesitate before saying he had excellent people; he just had to let go, take a little more risk, and trust and delegate.

For the next couple of weeks, Loretta and I had a trail of VPs visiting us to express their thanks for Loretta's great work. Bob had changed the entire process, with new delegations of authority such that the VPs could approve most AFEs, the CFO would have to approve all over a certain value, and Bob was only involved in truly major capital expenditures.

Incidentally, the story I told in Chapter 23 about Loretta having too much fun to leave the office at 7pm was during this project.

Surely, this is a story worth telling your grandchildren. It was "….dynamic, stimulating, a major bond builder among co-workers, a source of buzz among customers, and inspiring, exhausting, hot, cool, sexy, where everyone wants to be."

Chapter 28: Why do I need to write an audit report?

Patrick Sheehan, who led the internal audit team at Di Giorgio, taught me a number of lessons. One was my need to demonstrate empathy, which I wrote about earlier. He also demonstrated, through both words and actions, that he cared not only for the success of the company but for each of the members of his team. We loved him and readily followed him. Patrick was our leader.

Another lesson concerned audit reports.

The typical audit report had a number of standard sections, such as Scope and Objectives (which explained what we had audited), perhaps a Background section (describing the business and recent trends if we felt that information was not already known to our readers in management and on the board), and a Summary of Findings. That last section was essentially an executive summary of the results of our audit.

We used rating scales to communicate the significance of any "findings" or deficiencies in internal control (e.g., major, significant, or low risk) and our overall assessment of the adequacy of controls in managing the risks included in scope (e.g., satisfactory, needs improvement, or unsatisfactory).

Patrick taught me, the hard way, that simply putting text in these areas of the audit report was insufficient.

It is revealing that the IIA Standards do not require an audit report! Standard 2400, Communicating Results, simply says "Internal auditors must communicate the results of engagements."

The audit report, I learned, is not a document that summarizes what we did and shares what we would like to tell management and the board.

Instead, it is a communication vehicle. It is the traditional way internal audit communicates what management and the board *need to know about the results of our work.*

The audit report is not for our benefit as internal auditors. It is not a way to document our work and demonstrate how thorough we were. It is for the benefit of the readers of the report, management, and (when I was CAE) the audit committee. It tells them what they need to know, which is typically whether there is anything they need to worry about.

Standard 2420, Quality of Communications, says "Communications must be accurate, objective, clear, concise, constructive, complete, and timely". The Interpretation that follows has some powerful language, including these sentences:

> "Clear communications are easily understood and logical, avoiding unnecessary technical language and providing all significant and relevant information. Concise communications are to the point and avoid unnecessary elaboration, superfluous detail, redundancy, and wordiness. Constructive communications are helpful to the engagement client and the organization and lead to improvements where needed. Complete communications lack nothing that is essential to the target audience and include all significant and relevant information and observations to support recommendations and conclusions."

When I said that Patrick taught me the hard way, what I was referring to was that when it came time for me to write my first audit report (on information security at one of the divisions), he made me write and rewrite it until it was clear and concise – just as the above excerpt from the Standards requires.

Patrick wouldn't stop until my assessment and the issues I identified were clear and understandable, not to a technical IT person but to a lay business executive. It had to be written in simple English with a minimum of technobabble (i.e., limiting the use of technical terms).

About a week after the report was issued, I was in the San Francisco office and was surprised to be called in to see Bob Di Giorgio (our CEO). He thanked me and said that my audit report was "the first IT audit report I ever understood".

As the head of internal audit at Tosco, I wanted to build on what I had learned from Patrick.

I also wanted to apply a lesson I received while I was at Home Savings.

Mario Antoci, the President of the company, received a copy of our internal audit reports. He tasked his executive secretary with reading every report and highlighting the sections he needed to read. If there was nothing meriting his attention in the report, it was filed. If there were items of significance, she brought that to his attention straight away.

My initial thought was that I would highlight the audit reports for the board and top executives. But then I asked myself why the audit report had sections that they didn't need to read.

I talked to my key stakeholders in management and on the audit committee and listened carefully so I could understand what they needed to hear after an audit was completed.

I heard them say that they wanted to know the answers to two questions:

1. Is there anything they need to worry about?
2. Are there any issues of such significance that somebody in senior management should be monitoring how and when they are addressed?

In other words, they wanted to manage by exception. They were going to trust internal audit and operating management to address routine issues; they didn't want to waste their time (my expression; they didn't actually use those words) on matters that didn't merit their attention.

So, I designed a cover sheet for every audit report. It was simple and to the point. It looked like the example in Figure 2, below.

The members of my audit committees (starting with Tosco but continuing when the board members at my subsequent companies saw how easy it was for them to read them) wanted to receive a copy of each audit report at the time of its issue, even though by the time I left Tosco we were issuing a couple of hundred audit reports each year. Executive management similarly wanted to receive every audit reports.

All of these people are severely limited in the amount of time they can devote to reading audit reports, so it was up to me to ensure I communicated what they needed to know in a way that they could read and understand it quickly.

Figure 2: Audit Report Cover

January 15, 1995

Audit of Derivatives Trading

- Are there any risk issues of significance to the Audit Committee or executive management? YES/**NO**
- Are there any outstanding major internal control findings meriting Audit Committee or executive management attention? YES/**NO**

Distribution:
Audit Committee
Executive and Operating Management

The cover sheet was the first part of my answer to that question.

If either of the answers to the two questions on the cover page was "Yes", I would include a sentence (at most two) explaining the issue. Then they could read the rest of the report (or at least the Executive Summary) for more.

If the answers were both "No", unless they had a particular interest in the topic addressed by the audit, they might not read further – and they didn't need to.

∞

There was more that I wanted to do to make sure my audit reports were easy for board members and executives.

I wanted to avoid the need for anybody, including myself, to have to highlight what the executives and board members needed to read.

I wanted the audit report to be the highlighted content, with everything else either omitted or relegated either to the end of the report, included as an attachment, communicated in another way (e.g., to operating management at the closing meeting), or omitted entirely.

In other words, I wanted the executives to be able to read just the first 0few paragraphs and obtain the most critical information and satisfy their needs.

The first page of the audit report, behind the cover page described in Figure 2, is an Executive Summary and starts with the most important piece of information the executives needed to hear: our opinion on the adequacy of the controls over the risks included in our scope.

Figure 3 is the first part of the Executive Summary of a report from my team at Business Objects.

Figure 3: Audit Report Executive Summary

> In our opinion, adequate controls exist to ensure that the required level of approval is obtained when discounting license deals.
>
> However, there is no analysis detailing the discounts granted by deal, product, country, sales channel, etc. Without this discount reporting, it is nearly impossible to measure the financial impact of discounting on the Company or the effectiveness of our discounting strategy. A global discount report is being created detailing discounts granted by country, region, territory, sales rep, PLU for direct sales (Mid-Market and Enterprise) in both EMEA and Americas. The plan is to test and deploy the report in Q1 2008 and roll out to sales management in EMEA and Americas.

∞

The traditional way to express an opinion in an audit report is through a rating scale, such as one that uses a three point scale of Satisfactory, Needs Improvement, and Unsatisfactory.

I don't believe that a rating scale conveys to the executive reader what they need to know.

If we are tasked with assessing controls over risks, we should not only be telling management whether the risks are being managed effectively but explain, in business language, the effect on corporate objectives.

In Chapter 7, I told the story about how I asked Audrey Lee to explain what a draft audit report following her Shenzhen audit meant (see Figure 4). I asked her what she would tell the CEO if they were in an elevator and she said: "I would tell him that the controls in Shenzhen are not strong enough to support the planned 20% expansion of our business there."

This is providing management with the information they need to run the business. It was succinct and in business, not in audit language.

I left the table in, but the audit opinion – what Audrey told me – was up front and the first thing our executives read.

Figure 4: Illustrative Solectron Audit Report Table

Audit Area	Rating	Number of Significant Issues	Other Issues
General Accounting	●	3	5
Procurement	●	4	7
Inventory management	●	6	6
Employee health and safety	●	2	1
IT security	●	7	8
Customer billing	●	6	3
Code of conduct training	●	3	6

In those days, we mailed the audit reports. Later, we started sending them as attachments to emails.

I modified my approach to include the most critical information that I wanted all recipients to read in the email. If there were no issues meriting their attention, they could choose whether to download and read the attachment or not.

I recognized that if I made it easier and faster for time-strapped executives to receive the information they needed from me, they would be more likely to open and read the email. But, if they knew as they read the email only that there was an audit report attached, which might be many pages in length, they would probably defer reading until they "had time" (which sometimes was only over a weekend or when they were on a plane).

Figure 5, below, is an example of an email I sent to the executives and board members a few years later.

Figure 5: Example of an Emailed Audit Report

> To: Audit Committee, Executive and IT Management
> From: Norman Marks
> Subject: Information Security Foundations Audit Report
>
> This audit was designed to assess the information security foundations within XYZ. These are the foundations upon which a successful information security program can be built.
>
> Our assessment was not limited to the IT organization, but incorporated a review of the security processes within key business units (Product Group, Procurement, Legal, and Customer Advocacy) as they have direct accountability and responsibility for security within that group.
>
> The Information Security team is a newly reconstituted group within the IT organization that has purview for information security across all business and functional units within XYZ. Staffing for the security function started in January 200x and comprises five people, the last of whom joined the group in May 200x. As such, the team has only commenced their work and the current state of the information security environment should not necessarily be directly attributed to the team.
>
> In our opinion, the foundational Information Security processes are not sufficient to build a risk-based Information Security program. While there has been noticeable recent improvement in security mechanisms and processes (especially in the area of awareness, and in particular since the new head of information security was appointed), the establishment of an information security program that works effectively across the organization to meet the company's information security needs is at risk.
>
> Significant cross-functional responsibilities, processes, and security requirements remain undefined and pose a significant ongoing operational business risk.

∞

I recognized early on that I have multiple people to whom I needed to communicate the results of my team's work. In addition to the executive management team and the board, who wanted 'high level' information that might affect their work, I needed to share with operating management much more detail: what exactly was not working the way they wanted, and what should they do about it.

The first opportunity to communicate information that management needs to know is during the audit itself – when the issue or question first surfaces.

It is important to share these with operating management promptly, not only to confirm the facts, but to help them initiate corrective action quickly.

After all, we share the same goal: ensuring that risks are managed effectively.

We should not consider them and they should not consider us as adversaries.

Our goal should be to effect improvement, not to report as many issues as we can.

Frankly, I don't mind at all if management corrects issues before the report is issued. I will either drop the item from the report, especially if there is no need for executive management to know the weakness existed, or give management full credit for making the change.

By the way, I had an unsettling experience at an audit committee meeting (this was pre-SOX).

The external auditors shared information about the internal control weakness they had identified during their controls testing. They said that the risk from one of those weaknesses was fraud. However, I was not told about the weakness until just before the audit committee meeting – perhaps 8 weeks after their controls testing identified the issue.

I was not shy about sharing my views on the delay in informing me, as the head of the internal audit function, that there was a control weakness that represented a risk of fraud that the external auditors considered significant enough to report to the audit committee of the board.

The audit partner tried to tell me that he was not able to share the issue until the manager had reviewed the working papers and then discussed it with him; their standard process was for him to have that discussion of the results of testing only when the testing phase of the audit was finished.

I told him that was unacceptable and why. When I asked, he confirmed that operating management was also not informed until the week prior to the audit committee meeting, when the draft audit report was sent to them for comment.

When a control weakness opens the door to theft or fraud, management needs to know immediately so they can close it.

In the same way, we have an obligation to management to inform them of any risk or control concern as soon as possible so it can be addressed.

∞

The next opportunity is the closing meeting. This is a vitally important meeting where the audit team and management can review the results of the audit engagement; ensure a common understanding of the findings – the facts, what they mean to the business, the level of risk and whether it is acceptable; who will take action, if necessary, and what will they do by when.

Some issues, where the internal audit team believes that the risk is low, can be addressed by management at the closing meeting, and there is no need to inform more senior management or the board, I see no reason to include the issue in the audit report.

We don't keep score with the number of findings in the audit report, so why include low risk items in what we send to executive management and the board? I see no need.

Some issues and agreed action items need to be shared with senior management but don't merit the attention of executive management or the audit committee. I like to include these in a separate memo to management; I might make reference to this in the audit report, saying something like "Additional issues, not meriting the attention of executive management, have been shared in a separate memo to operating management."

My focus is always on providing each stakeholder with the information they need to run the business, when they need it, in a clear and easy-to-consume fashion.

∞

In today's environment, I am always looking for ways to use new technology to make internal audit communications more effective. One option is to find a way to integrate information about audit results into the dashboards and other information that management uses to run the business.

If they are getting key performance (and possibly risk) metrics on their tablets, why can't they also see – whenever they want it – the condition of risks and controls as reflected by our latest audit assessments? Why can't they see whether corrective actions are being made on a timely basis and which may be late?

One technique I have used, and I know a few others have as well, is to issue 'audit alerts' when we find an issue in one area of the business that might affect others. For example, if we find a defect in a report used by one location when we perform an audit there, we might share that information (without blaming anybody) with other locations that use that same report. There are a number of ways to do this. My team issued an email to those who needed to know; others might share the information using internal social media networks.

∞

There is one more topic to cover in this chapter: the difference between communicating the results from an assurance engagement and after a consulting or advisory engagement.

The primary customers for an assurance engagement are the board or audit committee, followed closely by executive and operating management. But the customers for a consulting or advisory engagement are in management.

Unless there is a risk or control issue that merits the attention of the board or individuals senior to my customer, I will find the best way to communicate the results to my customer (which might be in a formal audit report, a less formal memo, or an informal but documented meeting) and limit distribution to my customer. I might inform executive management and the board that I have performed a consulting engagement, but usually they don't need to be informed of the detailed results.

Chapter 29: Auditing forward

The definition of internal auditing from the IIA (emphasis added by me) is:

> "Internal auditing is an **independent, objective** assurance and consulting activity designed to add value and improve an organization's operations. It helps an organization accomplish its objectives by bringing a systematic, disciplined approach to **evaluate and improve the effectiveness of risk management, control and governance processes**".

I assess my effectiveness as CAE by my ability to prevent internal control or risk issues when I can, rather than identify them (and finding fault) when they already exist and represent an obstacle to organizational success.

If you are familiar with the CSI TV series, you can imagine a crime scene investigator entering a room and telling a detective "you have a dead body". If I can, I prefer to be working with management to ensure there are reasonable controls that would prevent a dead body.

That means a couple of things: seeing the value of internal audit as helping improve risk management and controls, and "auditing forward".

"Auditing forward" means being involved in new initiatives and projects (such as the pre-implementation controls review of a new IT system that Carla Williams led), providing consulting advice that helps management implement a reasonable level of controls and security.

It means seeing our success as linked to the success of management. If management implements a new system without sufficient controls or security, when we had an opportunity to warn them, it reflects as a failure on our part. Either we failed to identify the issue, to persuade management it was important, or to work with them on corrective actions that addressed the problem.

∞

At Tosco, the company embarked on a major initiative to implement the Oracle financial systems. With the full support of the audit committee and top management, I put my most senior people on the long project (it would last a few months). In addition to Lorie Reynolds and Tom Wisniewski, whom I knew I could rely on for quality work, I also assigned auditors such as Roger Herd who could bring an in-depth understanding of the business.

I remember calling a meeting to make sure everybody understood my thinking on the role they should play. I explained that while they should not make management decisions, they should do whatever it took short of that to help management understand potential risks and gaps in controls, and suggest how controls might be implemented (before the system went 'live') to address those risks.

I asked them what they would consider a successful internal audit engagement on this project. Their replies were all about providing key information to the project team, identifying potential problems and helping management resolve them.

I put a different 'spin' on what constitutes success.

I told them that if the project failed, whether from poor project management, inadequate user involvement, poor security or controls, or any other reason, I would not be able to call our involvement a success.

We would only call our involvement a success if the project itself was successful.

The team looked at me as if I was mad. I can still see their faces in my memory. But I held to my guns and told them that would be how I would evaluate them individually and as a team.

Fortunately, the team trusted me and adopted my approach. Also fortunately, the project was successful – and both I and senior company management recognized the team for their contributions.

∞

A few years later, Tosco's Circle K convenience store division embarked on a high risk (in my opinion) systems conversion. The company owned about 6,000 stores across the United States and did not believe its current systems would be able to continue to support the business.

The IT department worked with management of store operations and related departments in a disciplined process to identify their needs and select a solution they believed offered the best long-term capabilities.

When the project was given the go-ahead from executive management, together with a budget in excess of a million dollars for hardware, software, and consultants from Accenture, I again assigned some of my best people. Three IT audit managers (Tim Cox, Bruce Taylor, and Will Helton) were joined by an experienced audit manager (Jennifer Busch) with a business and financial focus.

They soon came to my office with shell-shock in their faces.

They asked me whether I knew what solutions the project team had selected. I didn't, so they told me.

The company was going to replace all the systems in the individual convenience stores. These ran the sales registers, maintained inventory and other records, and once or more each day uploaded information to the central system in our Phoenix data center. Both the hardware and the software were going to be replaced.

The software was designed for and used only by clothing boutiques in shopping malls. It had never been used in convenience stores.

It was going to run on hardware that it had never run on, and which also had never been used in a convenience store business.

There was no evidence, at least not to my team's satisfaction, that the hardware and software would work well together and be able to handle the volume in a typical convenience store.

As if this was not enough, the central system that collected data from the stores, was used by our Store Accounting staff to run reports analyzing the business, and then fed the financial and other enterprise applications, was also being replaced. This time, the software was one that had been used in a convenience store business but the hardware on which it was going to run had not – and the software had never run on that hardware.

The central system had never worked with the new store systems, of course.

As you can imagine, the audit team was very concerned. They believed, with every justification, that this was a project with a high risk of failure. Such a failure could have a massive effect on our business, effectively closing down our stores if things went badly.

I gave them my speech about their success being intertwined with the success of the project, and this was an opportunity to be of huge value to the company. They probably muttered to themselves about their mad manager, but they left determined and resolute.

During the course of the project, I was able to hire a highly technical IT auditor, Alan Proctor. This was fortunate as the project team had decided they needed to upgrade the security side of the central system. Alan not only provided technical insights they could use on the alternatives (he knew them, they didn't) but was also able to steer them in the right direction to avoid some of the potential security loopholes.

As the go-live date neared, my team asked to meet with me and discuss the situation.

Tim and Bruce spoke for the team when they said that there was a high risk that something would crash. It wasn't just a matter of controls and security. The size and scope of the entire system, when you consider the number of stores, the volume of transactions, and the fact that everything was new and the pieces had never been used in combination, was very complex.

The project team had not been able to test everything working together with anything like the volume of transactions that could be anticipated upon go-live.

Tim an Bruce believed that management should be informed that going live without additional testing in an environment more consistent with go-live conditions (i.e., with more realistic volumes) was high risk – in their view, unacceptably high risk.

I encouraged them to share this at the upcoming project steering committee meeting, when the CFO and CIO would be present. After they left, I made sure that the CFO and CIO knew that we had an important message to share and that the team would have sufficient time on the agenda.

I didn't attend the meeting myself (I trusted my team and had other matters to attend to), but my team did well. They informed me that top management had listened carefully; they had asked questions of the project team who had confirmed the facts upon which Tim, Bruce, and the others had based their assessment.

However, they considered not only the risk and cost of going forward with the implementation without delay, but the risk and cost of a postponement while they performed additional testing. Apparently, it would take some extended period of time for them to design a test environment with similar volumes as the live environment. In addition, they would have to extend any delay until after the year-end close – which would result in the loss of key consultants from Accenture.

The CFO and CIO decided to take the risk and forge ahead.

My team were downcast. However, we talked about what we could do to reduce the risk of a devastating crash and/or mitigate any damage.

They decided that they could identify the areas where the system was most likely to crash.

Brilliant! To this day, I am proud of this imaginative solution.

The team met with senior IT and project management to discuss which areas were most at risk. IT and users put people in place to monitor each of these high risk areas, with instructions on what to do should they fail.

As it happened, the new system failed in several areas – all of which had been predicted by the team! The prompt actions by the people watching these areas mitigated the damage to the extent that it was barely noticeable.

The overall project manager came into my office to tell me how grateful he was to everybody on the team, and to me for making them not only available but willing to do whatever they could to help the project succeed.

He was followed by the CIO. He told me that he would never again implement a major new system without first obtaining an assessment and advice from my team of IT auditors.

∞

"Auditing forward" also means auditing the risks that impact today and tomorrow, not limiting your focus to what has happened in the past.

Is there value in somebody telling you that the road in front of the house you lived in last year is being repaired? You only want to know about road conditions where you are likely to drive now or in the future.

In the same way, internal audit needs to provide assurance and consulting advice on the risks of today and tomorrow. Telling management what has been a problem in the past has some limited value, but only to the extent that those conditions continue to exist and similar problems may continue into the future.

Wayne Gretzky's father advised him to "skate where the puck's going, not where it's been".

Internal auditors need to take this advice to heart and audit where the risk is going to be, not where it has been.

That requires:

1. Being sufficiently agile to change the internal audit plan as risks and business conditions change; and,
2. Knowing that risks and business conditions are changing.

I have previously discussed my approach to audit planning, which I believe gives me the required agility.

Knowing that risks and business conditions are changing is achieved by meeting with all the key business leaders frequently and listening to what they have to say about the business, our competitors, changes in regulations, what is happening with customers and vendors, and much more.

I also attend the periodic meetings of the primary business units' executive teams – not so much to speak as to hear.

Finally, I receive a lot of information, such as copies of monthly operating reports and key metrics, so I can understand trends and know what questions to ask management. I may need to supplement the information management receives with my own analytics. For example, at Business Objects my team developed reports using the company's analytics software that told me when the risk of revenue-related accounting fraud was high.

Business leaders and the board like it when internal auditors talk about the business using the language of the business; when we can demonstrate that we understand what the company is doing and where it wants to go; and, where we can show that our work is directed to helping them succeed – arriving safely where they want to go.

Chapter 30: Effecting change

Some CAEs measure the effectiveness of the internal audit function with metrics such as the number of recommendations made (and perhaps their severity) and the percentage of findings accepted by management.

Neither of these work for me.

If you have an effective internal audit department, you should be finding any serious issues the first time you audit an area. You should also be working with management to get the necessary corrective actions taken.

If the number of audit findings does not diminish over time, something is wrong. Certainly, something is wrong with management's ability to maintain effective systems of risk management and internal control.

But has internal audit been effective in identifying the correct root cause and actions necessary to fix the problem? Has it been effective in communicating this to management and persuading them that the risk is not acceptable?

Or does internal audit continue to identify issues that management does not believe merit action?

If the CAE reports that 90% of audit recommendations are accepted by management, that means that 10% are not. Who is willing to accept a 10% defect rate? Not I!

We should measure quality through the change that is made, which goes even further than whether the recommendation is made because it talks to the recommendation being implemented.

An effective internal audit department should see consistent improvement in management's risk and control systems, meaning that the number of findings – especially significant ones – diminishes.

At Tosco, we started with an environment with somewhat shaky systems. First, we audited the core systems like accounts payable, general ledger, and so on. As those improved and related risks diminished, we moved to areas such as environmental compliance and refinery operations. Those also improved and we became more of a consulting organization, because the areas where there were the greatest risks were where there were changes – such as new systems, acquisitions, and so on. In other words, we became more proactive.

I believe our effective internal audit team helped the company minimize risk and control issues.

∞

I believe a world-class internal audit function not only audits forward and helps the organization avoid issues, but is focused on enabling the organization to take corrective actions when they are required.

One of the first IT audits that Lorie did for me at Tosco was of the contingency plans for the Northern California data center. Her budget was 100 hours and I checked in with her to see how she was doing after a couple of weeks. She shook her head in reply and sighed, "not very well, Norman. I am going to need at least another couple of weeks before I can finish the audit and give you a report to close." I asked her why and she explained that she had found so many problems that it would take her that long just to make sure she had them all, could review them with the local CIO, and agree on corrective action.

My reply was that I thought she had finished the audit.

Lorie looked at me in shock. I explained that from what she was telling me, she had already completed her assessment: the contingency plan was inadequate and major work was needed. She agreed with the assessment but repeated that she needed the extra hours to write the report, define the actions necessary, and obtain management responses.

I told her "No. You can finish the audit by writing the audit report with just one finding: the contingency plan needs to be fixed. But I will give you an extra month to work with the CIO on a consulting engagement, helping him figure our precisely how to make that fix."

Lorie took that idea to the CIO who loved it, as did senior management.

Our focus on working with management to effect change, rather than writing an audit report and getting management responses, was warmly welcomed and the plan was updated promptly. Not only that, but Lorie was able to help them implement a process to maintain the plan so that it remained current.

When internal audit is effective, you get a positive answer to the question "Does internal audit help you identify the need for change and improvement in the business, and then to get those changes made?

Chapter 31: Leadership

A leader is somebody who is followed.

You don't get to be a leader through position alone. You need to have people believe you know where you are going and they need to have confidence that you will get there.

They also need to believe it is in their best interests to join you (that may be because they will reap rewards as you succeed; it may be because they are learning and growing; and it could be because we have a lot of fun.)

Those that follow you do so because they trust in you as a leader and especially in your integrity. This has to be more than words; it has to be something that is essential to who you are and how you behave.

Many years ago I was told that you cannot fake who you are. People will see right through you. So I have tried to be the best Norman Marks I can be. I believe that all people deserve our respect and try at all times to give it. I haven't always succeeded, but that ethos has been how I have lived my life – and continues to be how I try to live in my retirement.

I think the fact that I have shown respect, listened to people, and honestly wanted them all to grow and succeed, have helped me not only bring out the best from my people, but has allowed me to gain their respect as well as that of my peers and managers.

If I have been successful, it is due entirely to the great work of so many great people whom I have been honored to have on my teams over the years. Many of them have been mentioned earlier in the book and I have named as many as I can at the end of the book.

Some have been gracious enough to share their thoughts on what it was like working in an internal audit team where I was the CAE.

Rosnah Ismael was an audit manager in Singapore when I was the Vice President, Internal Controls and Process Assurance at Maxtor. These are her words:

"Norman is a boss whom I respect and fear too. I respect him for his knowledge yet fear to disappoint him with the quality of my work. Therefore each time before I submit my work to him, I will go through it more than five times to make sure that I don't have any silly mistakes and address all those that need to be addressed. However in my short two years working with him, he has never once made me feel that I am not good enough. He is able to make me want to give my best without having to be a fierce superior. He was always there to guide but not spoon-feed us and therefore he made us think and push us to go out of our comfort zone. Even though Norman and I are not in the same office, he is based in our US office and I am based in the Singapore office, this does not impose any problem if I need to contact him. He will reply to all our emails almost immediately regardless of time and this makes me wonder if he ever sleeps. If I have to relive my life again, I would like to work with Norman again from the start of my career so that I can get a good head start in my career development under his mentorship."

What I love about this, apart from the memories of working with this fine lady, is that she recognizes that I am always trying to make her (and everybody else) think. If I always give my answer to a question from one of my team, how can I expect them to learn to think for themselves? They almost always have the answer within them; I just have to help them see it for themselves. That remains my objective when I write, blog, and speak. It doesn't matter whether everybody agrees with me, as long as I make them think!

∞

Cary Morgan ran the Sarbanes-Oxley compliance program for me at Business Objects. He later stepped up to run the internal controls program for SAP (including SOX but his responsibilities included internal controls for all objectives, not only external financial reporting) after they bought Business Objects. He saw me as his teacher and mentor:

> "You provided me the opportunity to learn. You allowed me to grow in areas of responsibility and held me accountable for my actions. When correction was needed you asked questions that lead me to the proper solution rather than dictating the answer. You encouraged me to contribute to the team and allowed me to be recognized for my achievements without overshadowing with your presence.
>
> "Example: When I first met you I was operating under the mindset of PCAOB Auditing Standard No. 2 – catch everything in a tight net and then weed out what you didn't need. You quickly saw the financial benefits to Business Objects of early adoption of PCAOB Auditing Standard No. 5 (AS 5) and evangelized the "top down, risk-based approach". You taught us (we were pretty much all a new team back then) the mantra of "Is this control precise enough to detect or prevent a material error?" If not, is it needed? Does it need to be refined?
>
> "We didn't need any external training or coaching on AS 5. You were the trainer. Training sessions were question and answer sessions. You taught me how to think and ask reasonable questions to arrive at a logical conclusion. We had only known each other for a month or so and I was still a contractor when you put me in charge of coordinating the worldwide SOX 404 process for Business Objects. No doubt that was a bit of a leap of faith on your part, but I appreciated you allowing me to contribute to not only the team, but to Business Objects even though I was still an "outsider" at the time."

I am proud of Cary. Senior SAP management was sufficiently impressed by his SOX and leadership abilities that they moved him to Germany to run both the SOX and internal controls programs for the company.

Ivy Yeo, who was an audit manager in Singapore with Rosnah, also comments on my ability as a teacher:

> "You are the best teacher in my life! You just know when is the time to give me a straight answer to my question (for questions which are beyond my ability to solve). You know just when is the time to answer my question with another question to stretch my ability to think further and discover the answers on my own. My life is never quite the same after working for you. You continued to help me out after I left Maxtor. You remained the best teacher in my life :)"

I like to think that I hire the best, mentor them as needed, and then get out of their way.

I insist that everybody learns to think for themselves. For example, I find that the people I hire straight out of public accounting (even those in the internal audit services side of the accounting firm) have been trained <u>not</u> to think. They have been trained to follow the directions of their manager and in the audit program, and not to exercise any independent thinking of their own. One of my first tasks with these people is to teach them to question everything and use their intelligence, intellect, curiosity, and imagination as tools for success.

A leader is someone who is followed. Lorie Reynolds, who worked for me at Tosco, Maxtor (as a consultant), and then Business Objects focused on that and how I always asked her to stretch herself:

> "I have had the pleasure of working for Norman Marks for 11 of the 24 years that I have known him. During this time, Norman's relentless pursuit of making himself the best leader put him in front of the crowd. I know that there are those of us that have worked for him that would work for him again – anytime and anywhere – and some of us have shown that.
>
> "Throughout the years, I have had many bosses and only two of those were true leaders. Norman was one of them. There's a clear difference between being a boss and a leader. A leader is a motivation for others and inspires individuals to aim high and

attain that aim. However a boss only supervises his subordinates. Norman has high expectations from the people that work for him. For instance, he knew my capabilities better than I knew myself; he challenged me beyond my comfort level and then pushed me to my maximum potential."

I mentioned Tim Cox back in Chapter 29. This is what he shared:

> "It was my pleasure to work with you, even for the few years that I was at Tosco prior to the acquisition. The thing that always stands out in my mind was your placement of trust in those you hired. You provide full support, even in the toughest of times. I remember when the new inventory control system (name escapes me) was going on. While the company had hired a big-name consulting firm to play a big role in the project, they did not have the expertise nor drive to be as efficient and effective in collecting and documenting our business requirements. The requirements were written so loosely that they could be easily misinterpreted and that turned out to be one of the downfalls of the project. I remember how much you supported our project audit team, and how you would learn all that you could, never doubting us, so that you too could relay a consistent message to senior management. I have not seen nor felt such management support before or since that time. That is why, when Tosco was sold, it was truly heart-breaking to me to have to leave that environment. I still look back with fond memories of those days."

Tim doesn't give himself enough credit. He was a leader on the project he mentions and which I described in Chapter 29. He was not only trusted by me and the rest of the team, but by IT and the project team. Why? Because he was straightforward at all times, dedicated to the success of the organization, and performed brilliantly.

In other words, he was easy to trust.

∞

Marty Patton is an alumnus and a successful CAE. He had different insights on my leadership style.

> "I was afforded the opportunity to know and work for Norman for almost 20 years. My work experience with Norman included Tosco Refining Company and Solectron. Under Norman's leadership both audit departments were considered World Class. Literature says leadership style is the manner and approach of providing direction, implementing plans, and motivating people. Norman had an unique leadership philosophy where he adapted to the demands of the situation, the abilities of the staff and the needs of the organization. He was able to move between leadership styles utilizing the one needed for the challenges that the company was facing. He was at times visionary along with a coaching emphasis while not micromanaging. Norman set high standards, was democratic but occasionally would utilize a classic authoritarian style when needed with certain employees and situations. Norman moved easily between leadership styles which resulted in developing World Class departments. As the Chief Audit Executive for a semiconductor company I still consult Norman on various audit topics and practice leadership techniques I learned under his tutelage."

∞

Katie Vo worked with me at Maxtor and then at Business Objects. She had some kinds words to share about **trust** and **loyalty.**

> "*Trust* – We all know that Norman is confident (not arrogant) and intelligent. Trust is not about only confidence or intelligence, but more about being fair and honest to the people that he associates with. He is always fair to his employees and I have never seen him

demonstrate favoritism to anyone. He is honest and direct to the point. Sugarcoating is non-existent in his vocabulary. When I first met Norman, I was intimidated by his intelligence. My fear was 'would this man make me feel stupid every day?' As a matter of fact, I wasn't sure if he would even hire someone like me. However, that is just the surface. The real Norman is more than just confident and intelligent. He is a good person all around. He does not come to work with a personal agenda. Modern day business leaders tend to put their own interests ahead of the organization. He's a firm believer that you are hired to do what is best for the Company and he will give you the tools to ensure that you are successful. This is the tone that he has set and communicated with this to his team from the very beginning. A character trait that truly defines Norman is that he generously gives 'trust' to everyone. From the projects he assigns to his team to the decisions they have to make on a daily basis, Norman always trusts that his team will do what is right and in the best interest for the Company. The relationship that Norman has built with his team is founded on trust and communications.

"**Loyalty** – Norman is exception at building great teams. He knows how to put together a strong team that is cohesive and collaborative. He knows what motivates his staff and where they want to go in their careers. He understands their strengths and weaknesses and always put them in a position to succeed, to be challenged, but not to fail. Leaders who have too much power and move up the corporate ladders too quickly tend to lose the most important quality in them, their humanity. Whether work or personal matters, I could always reach out to Norman at ANY hours of the day. Norman will always listen and give you his honest unfiltered opinion. If he doesn't know the answer, he will admit that he doesn't know or when he is challenged and he's wrong, he will take responsibility and quickly act to improve. Norman will always there for his employees, to ensure that they are well taken care of in any situation. I've been through two acquisitions with Norman and both times he has gone the extra mile to make sure that his employees are taken care of, especially in situations of uncertainty. These are very special traits that one cannot develop overnight and it is why employees are naturally drawn to him for inspiration and guidance."

When I hired Teo Han Kheng as an audit manager in Singapore with Maxtor, she was only in her twenties. But she had the presence and attitude of a natural leader. I am proud of what she has to say:

"What makes a good leader? Norman comes to mind - being able to motivate team members to excel and perform at their best, feel taken care of for their development and welfare, and most importantly, constantly thinking and learning. A good leader need not have no faults, but should still garner everyone's respect despite not being perfect."

That's a great note on which to leave this chapter.

Chapter 32: Working with difficult people

In chapter 8, I talked about how David Clark shocked me when he said that one of the senior managers thought I was arrogant.

My immediate reaction was defensive on three counts: the accusation of being arrogant was wrong because I am naturally shy and somewhat afraid of authority figures; the person making the accusation was somebody who had clearly taken a personal dislike to me; and, the senior manager had made the accusation because I knew more than he did and he felt threatened by me.

But David guided me to understand that I had left this senior manager, and others, with the perception that I was arrogant. My self-confidence and belief that I was leading the way to understanding IT general controls, when expressed by somebody so young and junior, needed to be more restrained.

He also helped me understand that whatever I did there would always be people who didn't like me or for other reasons were difficult to work with.

I have had to work with difficult people all my life, whether in personal or work situations.

The early lessons I received (especially relating to humility) helped me see that I were to be successful I would have to learn how to work effectively with difficult people.

Sometimes, those difficult people literally held the keys to my success in their hands – as I worked for them. At other times, I had to obtain information people were reluctant to provide; I needed to persuade executives that they should work with me as the internal auditor; and, if I were to add value and effect change, people had to be persuaded to listen to and consider my recommendations and assessments.

That senior computer audit manager in the UK was one of the first situations where I had to find a way to work with a difficult person. As David pointed out to me, he was not only a senior manager (at that time , two levels above me) but probably the second most senior person below partner in the UK computer audit practice. He was influential, with the ear of partners and the potential to join their ranks.

I didn't want to do it, but I called the senior manager and apologized for appearing arrogant. I told him that I didn't realize that I was making that impression on him and others, and that I recognized that he was not only senior to me but far more experienced.

He told me that he appreciated my call and there were no further unpleasant experiences; fortunately, I didn't have to work with him very often.

Sometimes, there is nothing you can do.

David had urged me to find a way to go to the States so some of the Americans' charisma would rub off on me. The UK firm had shut down the exchange program they had run for several years with the US firm, where each would send to the other a promising manager for a period of six months or so. The reason was that almost all of the people sent to the US never came back! With David's support, I contacted the US partners I had worked with on the IT general controls project and they agreed to bring me over for six months in their Atlanta office.

The UK firm agreed to the temporary move. Before I left, I met with one of the senior UK computer audit partners. He asked for and received a promise from me that I would return, and told me that he expected that when I returned I would be promoted to senior manager and given charge of the London office (the largest computer audit office in the global firm).

While I was away, the second most senior audit partner in the UK firm (whom I had never met) decided that a change was needed in the leadership of the computer audit group and was able to move somebody who had worked extensively for him into leadership of the London office computer audit group. I knew the lady, considered her a friend, and knew she was very well qualified to lead the group.

One of the UK computer audit partners (Rod Perry) made a point of meeting with me in New York (where I had started, with UK approval, a three month extension to work with the US national office on controls in a database environment). He told me that this was no reflection on me. On the contrary, he had received glowing reports from the US firm and he and the other partners still thought highly of me. He told me that they would find a good position for me when I returned to London. I trusted him because of his openness and knew that he was the partner running the UK computer audit practice day-to-day.

I kept my promise, despite tempting offers to stay in the US, and returned to London. I was immediately promoted to senior manager, one of the youngest to hold that position.

But the position they offered me was as the technical computer audit senior manager, with a staff of perhaps one person. This was essentially the role that I had been playing before I left for the States. It was also the position that David Clark had told me would never lead to partnership.

I asked for and was granted a meeting with the same senior computer audit partner I had met before I left. I told him that the technical computer audit role was one I had held for some time and would not provide me the learning and growth opportunity. I asked if there was another opportunity for me where I could be of value to the firm and at the same time advance my career.

The partner lost his composure. He told me that I was an ingrate. They had made me a senior manager, even though I was not that great an auditor. If I didn't like the position, I should resign.

I was shocked but kept my own composure. I thanked him for his time and left.

After I settled down, I went to see the partner I had met in New York. He was as shocked as I at the senior partner's reaction. He was quick to calm me and assure me that I was very highly rated within the firm (later, I found out that I had been earmarked as having the potential to move up to partner). He suggested I give him some time and not make any precipitative move, such as resigning.

I waited several weeks and then decided to ask the senior partner to meet me for lunch. I was pleased when he agreed.

But he surprised me at lunch by accusing me and the US firm of underhand behavior. He said that he "knew" that I had already accepted a position in the New York office and refused to listen to my denials.

Shortly thereafter, I called Stan (the US partner in charge of the computer audit practice) to warn him. He told me that should I need to leave the UK firm I should call him – but not before then, otherwise people would accept the accusations as true.

A few weeks later, I saw the senior partner from a distance. My blood boiled just looking at him. I knew he was there to stay, so I had to leave.

After I resigned, I received a letter from the partner in charge of the UK firm's HR function. He told me that he was very disappointed in my lack of loyalty to the firm, demonstrated by accepting an offer from the US firm before I returned to the UK.

I replied without much hope. I recognized that the poison spread by the senior partner would stick. Why he did it, I don't know.

Fortunately, Stan kept his word and I was able to join the Los Angeles office as the manager in charge of their computer audit team.

But I inherited another difficult set of individuals there!

∞

I worked with some great people at Coopers & Lybrand in their Los Angeles office. But the culture was not positive. I understand that what I encountered was localized and doesn't persist today, but in those days many of the partners and all the managers working to become partners were highly political.

What we might call "dirty tricks" were not uncommon. One aspiring senior manager told me that he joined every committee he could and claimed ownership of every achievement by that group, even if he had nothing to do with it. He cozied up (there are less pleasant phrases) to every partner so he could get their vote, making sure they knew how great he was even if he never worked with them.

A partner told me that I should always try to sell services to a customer (internal or external) even when I knew they didn't need those services.

My group manager told partners I was stealing work from another manager, when the truth was that he had decided (against my recommendation) to give the assignment to me because the client liked me. That group manager said this to discredit me because he thought I was a threat to him and his prospects.

Clearly there was no way I was going to change this environment. It was also clear to me that I didn't belong.

My personal belief structure, my ethics, prevent me from being anything other than honest and straightforward.

With the support of my family, for which I am grateful, I left a position where the leadership of the firm had assured me I would make partner.

There are some people that are so difficult to work with that it is necessary to leave.

But there were also situations where I was able to change a difficult situation and make progress.

∞

While I was at Coopers & Lybrand, I took a course on dealing with difficult people. I would recommend this to anybody and feel that I learned a great deal from the instructor.

For example, I learned to let an angry person talk, while I listened actively and attentively, until they had said everything they needed to say. I would prompt them with questions to ensure they had said everything and were not holding anything back. It is important to everybody to be heard, and that alone can calm people down. David Augsburger said "Being heard is so close to being loved that for the average person they are almost indistinguishable".

I make sure that I let angry people know that I have not only heard but understand their position. In addition to making the individual more receptive, it gives me the information I need before I can respond. Sometimes, they say something that is news to me – even to the point where they have good reason to complain!

Until I am sure I understand their position, I can't respond to it! If I reply without thinking about what they have said, they will correctly conclude that not only have I not listened to what they have to say but that I don't care!

I always try to be professional and polite. There is little to be gained by telling people they are wrong, ignorant, and silly – or worse. All that will do is inflame the situation and make it impossible to work with them in a constructive fashion.

∞

Over the years I have worked effectively with people that I dislike, including some that I did not think were ethical, competent, or able to think logically. But, I worked hard not to let them know how I felt.

For example, when I joined one company (which I will not name, for obvious reasons), I knew the executive that I would be reporting to. I had worked within his organization, although not directly for him, for several years and knew that he could be a bully. But, I needed the job and apart from him the opportunity was excellent – a fine company and an interesting position.

I set myself a two-part goal. The first part was never to let him know that while I respected his intellect and experience, I didn't like him as a human being. The second part was that I wanted him to both like me and respect me for my work.

Unfortunately, I didn't work for him for long (both of our positions were outsourced). But at the end I knew that I had succeeded; he recommended to the CFO that he find a position for me within his team.

∞

One executive for whom I had great respect, as a professional and a human being, was Dave Wagner at Home Savings. I had only had periodic and limited conversations with him (including the incident described in chapter 17) when I was the leader of the IT audit function and he ran all the bank's application development and maintenance teams. Then, he was appointed acting CIO.

When I started the operational audit of IT that I mentioned in chapter 17, Ted Tomlinson was the CIO and a gentleman I liked and respected. He was always ready with an open door as well as an open mind when I needed to discuss an audit, his plans for the department, and so on.

But when it was time for me to meet with Ted to closing the operational audit, he didn't return my calls. When I stopped by his office, either it was empty or his secretary told me he was in a meeting.

Then I heard that he had resigned and was leaving the company. Dave was appointed acting CIO and his assistant readily scheduled a meeting so I could close the audit with him. Dave already had a copy of the draft audit report, as I had copied him when I sent the draft to Ted.

When I sat down with Dave in his new office, we chatted warmly about Ted leaving and giving Dave a "mess" to fix – including closing my audit. I told Dave that Ted had avoided my calls to meet and discuss the audit report. Dave laughed and said that when he read the draft he could see why Ted not only had dodged me but left the company!

Almost as soon as I started talking about the audit, explaining that it was an operational audit, Dave jumped in. He changed his smile to a snarl and told me:

> "If you are going to do this type of audit, telling me whether the department is efficient and what I need to fix, you should be sitting in this chair and not me!"

I may have started to smile at what I hoped was a joke, but quickly realized it was not. Instead, I asked him to tell me why he thought that way. I was using the techniques I had learned in the 'dealing with difficult people' class. I drew him out and showed that I understood where he was coming from. I understood his perspective and that he had not experienced an operational audit before.

Then I explained that in no way was I trying to run IT. My purpose was to provide him with information that would make him more successful. It was an independent and objective look at the operation by somebody who had experience in many IT departments in many industries over quite a few years.

He grunted an acknowledgement and agreed to talk about and consider what I had found.

In the end, he acknowledged that not only were my thoughts, as reflected in the draft, factually correct but that they would provide him useful information as he made adjustments to the department. In fact, some of my recommendations were actions that he had already decided to take. My audit report would encourage executive management to support his plans.

Dave and I had a great relationship after that. After I had moved out of internal audit and into IT, I had the opportunity to work for him – an opportunity to realize how fine an individual he was.

As an aside, when I was on his team, Dave had weekly meetings with his direct reports (of which I was one). He would dole out assignments and they always seemed to come to me. One week, I told him that I had a lot on my plate and perhaps somebody else would appreciate the "opportunity" he had just handed me (I used that word with a smile). Dave smiled back and told me I should feel complimented by his giving me so many opportunities.

∞

Be professional, patient, listen, and show respect. These are the primary techniques I use when dealing with difficult people.

It helps enormously to recognize that difficult people usually have a reason for being difficult.

Sometimes, it is because they have something to hide. That is the normal reaction of internal auditors when they feel their customer is withholding information or access, avoiding them, and so on.

But more often there is a valid reason – at least in the eyes of the problem manager.

For example, when I was at Solectron management of our Malaysia operations was more than just difficult to work with. They were nigh on impossible to work with!

Chapter 33: Working with a difficult region

When I started with Solectron as the Vice President, Internal Audit, my regional internal audit director, Audrey, told me that I needed to get approval from local management before I could schedule an audit of one of their facilities. At first, I thought she was referring to the need, with which I concurred, to agree on the timing of our audit. But no, she meant that we needed management permission to do the audit at all!

It took a visit to the region and a meeting with the Asia Pacific President and his number two, who ran the Malaysia operations, to change expectations. The president, Chester Lin, threw his full support behind me. He made it clear that internal audit was independent and was to be given full access and full cooperation.

That doesn't mean everything went smoothly – far from it!

For a while, the audits went well although it was always hard getting agreement on any issues we might find. Issues were generally small, and I found out one of the reasons why – the Malaysia operations team performed their own audits (they had a Certified Internal Auditor on their finance staff) before we arrived, so they could clean up before we found anything.

When I tried to persuade them that this was a waste of time and resources, I found that their bonuses were tied to the number and severity of any findings included in our audit reports.

The other main reason was that the management and staff at the Malaysian facilities (in and around Penang) were first class. They were disciplined, aggressive in obtaining quality materials at low prices, and generally in providing customers with the products they needed when they needed them.

Although operations were top-notch and internal controls and risk management generally in good shape, the Penang operation was the largest in the Solectron global empire. So, in spite of their management's wishes, these facilities always ranked high in our audit (later, risk) universe. They believed that out audits were not helping them, a distraction and disturbance, and that we should audit where people were losing rather than making money.

So when, with executive management agreement, I determined that one of the most significant risks for the company as a whole was our ability to procure quality materials at a good price from reliable vendors who delivered on time, Penang was firmly in my sights.

It was not a target, per se. I wanted to include Penang in the audit because I expected that we would find world-class ideas and practices that we could ensure were shared with our other facilities.

When I met with the corporate Executive Vice President responsible for procurement and logistics, he was not only highly supportive of the audit but keen to show us what we would now call an entity-level monitoring control. His team used analytics to chart actual prices obtained for raw materials, by product and facility, against the prices he had agreed with our primary vendors in global contracts.

Figure 6: Monitoring of material prices

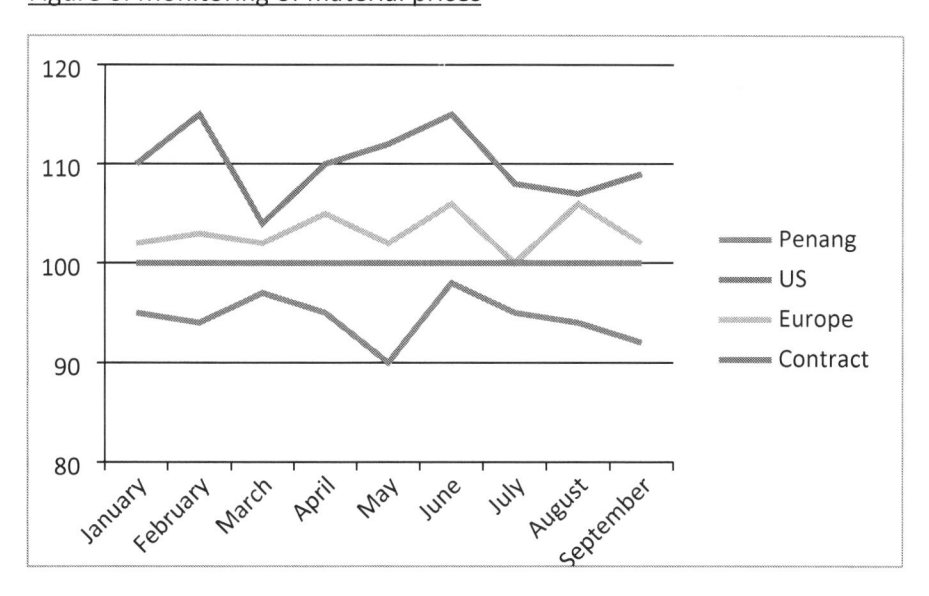

Figure 6 is representative of what he showed me. He had charts like this for every global contract, with similar results.

My reaction was that it supported my impressions of the effectiveness of the operations teams in different parts of the world: US operations were not obtaining the best price, Europe was doing better, and Penang was world class.

But the EVP blew me away when he said his problem was with Penang!

He tolerated the US and Europe results, saying he could explain their variances away due to premiums for delivery and so on. (I thought the explanations weak.)

But he said that Penang was ignoring the global contracts he and his corporate team had negotiated. Instead they were driving hard and aggressive deals with local dealers and subsidiaries (for exactly the same materials), and this was putting his global contracts at risk.

I told him I understood and we would consider that in our audit.

But, I knew that our margins were tiny and a small difference in the price we obtained for key materials could make the difference between profit and loss. I expected to find practices in Penang that the others should adopt, not practices we should stop them from doing.

With his concurrence, I decided that our audit would include visits to four locations: Charlotte (probably the best run US operation); Bordeaux (probably the best in Europe; Penang; and Suzhou, China (rapidly becoming our largest operation).

I put together a 'dream team' of auditors: Audrey Lee (Asia Pacific director), Shelley Hobbs (Americas director), and Mike Wilmouth (my expert in procurement and contracts auditing). Their schedule was to visit Penang first, to see how our best procurement team worked, then go to Suzhou, Bordeaux, and finish with Charlotte.

We went through the normal processes of sharing with each site our audit plans and schedule. As normal, Penang was difficult to deal with (slow to respond) but we settled on a date for the audit to start.

I was at home watching TV with my family when I received a call. It was Shelley, telling me that Penang was not permitting them to do the audit!

Audrey and Mike confirmed that when they arrived at the main office in Penang, they were not allowed beyond the lobby. They were told by the financial controller that because management had not agreed to the audit, it could not proceed. After arguments, they were permitted to enter and use a conference room. But neither the facility general manager nor the vice president in charge of procurement would meet or even talk to them by phone.

I tried calling but was not able to reach any of the executives in Asia, so I sent the regional president and the Penang management head urgent emails and told the team to do what they could. I would talk to the corporate executives in the morning (US west coast time).

In the morning, I talked to the corporate executive vice president for procurement. He was astonished and tried calling Penang, but his vice president wouldn't take his calls either! He sent emails and left voice messages without any response.

Eventually, the cooler heads in regional management prevailed and instructed Penang to cooperate. They did and we were able to complete the audit as planned.

The only comments we included in the final audit report relating to Penang were, as we had anticipated, complimentary.

We did not take issue with their working hard to get better prices, as we all felt the corporate team in the US had not negotiated effectively and it was more important to focus on upgrading those efforts than blaming Penang procurement for doing what was, overall, best for the company.

I don't know for sure whether this very rough patch helped or hindered our relationship with Penang. But I have to think that the fact that we never lost our cool, always acted professionally, and didn't try to get the Penang management team disciplined, helped our cause.

∞

A year or so later, we had an amusing incident on an audit where the tide finally turned.

Wendy Ng led the audit, which included a look at segregation of duties in the accounts payable area. Although she was a financial rather than an IT auditor, she found that one supervisor not only had access to enter and approve purchase orders, but could process receipts and approve payments. Not a good situation!

At my request, Wendy and the team checked and were able to confirm by inspecting transaction records that the supervisor had not exercised any of the additional capabilities. She had never accepted a receipt nor had she approved a payment – both of which were outside her job responsibilities.

Wendy met with the manager in IT responsible for the application systems involved. For a few days, the manager tried to persuade Wendy that she was wrong and that the supervisor did not have the rights in question. It took a call from me to the CIO for Asia Pacific before IT confirmed the facts and acknowledged that Wendy was correct.

The IT manager told Wendy that although the supervisor had the rights, they had an effective control in place.

What was that control?

> "We don't tell people that they have any additional capabilities. We only tell them what they need to know."

She wouldn't change her position, so it fell to me again to talk to the CIO for Asia Pacific.

In the end, we were able to come to an agreement. The weakness existed; it had not been utilized to commit a fraud; Penang did not have an effective control in place; and, management did not have an easy solution.

The application in question was software that had been acquired from a small Asian vendor and was no longer supported. It would be difficult and, in IT's estimation, expensive to change the way that the software worked so they could limit individuals to the access they needed for their responsibilities.

We agreed that our report would identify the weakness and that management would respond that they believed the cost of corrective action would exceed the level of risk. We would leave the decision to corporate management and, if necessary, the audit committee of the board as to whether they would accept Penang management's response.

I came out to Penang for the closing meeting, ably led by Wendy. The IT issue was covered with no problem, but there were other issues that the team had identified. These were significant from an operational point of view; management agreed with the facts and told us they would respond with their planned corrective actions shortly.

As I was walking out of the conference room after the meeting, I turned around to congratulate Wendy for her controlled, composed leadership. Before I could say much though, I heard my name called behind me.

I turned around to see the Penang controller and CIO. They asked for a moment with Wendy and me. Then came words I would never have believed I would hear:

> "Norman, we don't think we can solve our problems alone. Can you have Wendy come and work with us so we can fix everything?"

In the end, our ability to effect constructive change, with business-practical assessments and recommendations, allied with our professional manner, brought Penang around.

When I left Solectron, I was pleasantly surprised to receive invitations to connect on LinkedIn from two of the key members of the Penang management team: the senior executive for the region and the CIO.

Chapter 34: Organizational culture

One of the areas of internal control that every CAE should be concerned with is the culture of the organization.

Some talk about the "tone at the top", but equally if not more important are the "tone in the middle" and the "tone in the trenches".

In other words, we should worry about how people behave at all levels of the organization.

Is there a culture of integrity?

Is there a culture where risk and uncertainty are given appropriate attention?

Is there a culture that is conducive to realizing the potential for the organization to deliver value to its stakeholders?

I have worked in organizations that had great and others that had questionable culture. Often, the culture was not consistent across the organization, with some areas much healthier than others.

I have also seen situations where top management was excellent but there were problems in middle management. For example, I would place the senior management at Tosco in the top tier, but that didn't prevent us from finding many instances of fraud involving middle management – concentrated in Florida, for some reason.

At Business Objects, John Schwarz was the CEO and he wanted to make sure that everybody in Finance, especially those in our regional offices, knew that he counted on their integrity and ability to speak up when there was any doubt about the accounting. We had a quarterly meeting of the senior executives to review the system of internal controls and the quality of the financial statements we planned to file with the S.E.C. He called each regional controller personally, without the CFO present, to ask them about the quarterly report and their confidence in our controls and the numbers. I think that was magnificent.

I consider the CEO at Maxtor, C.S. Park, a man of immense personal integrity. When the company started losing money, he held an all-hands meeting. After explaining the difficult situation, he told us that we would have to let some people go.

He apologized for management's failures to prevent this! He and the company president then announced that they would take significant reductions in their compensation until the company returned to profits. This contrasts with the CEO at another company I worked at who took a bonus for his work in laying people off - and spent a million dollars refitting the executive office suite.

∞

When there are problems with culture, such as when multiple frauds surface and those involved claim that they believed they were expected to "find a way to make the numbers", the CAE has to stand tall.

Giving the audit committee the bad news that there is an issue with the organization's culture is hard. The CAE knows that unless he is very careful (and lucky), this can be a "career limiting move" – if not the end of his time with the company.

It is easy to say that the CAE reports to the audit committee and not to management. But when the CEO and/or the CFO wants the CAE fired, which can happen when the CAE reports bad news, the CAE has to be brave. (I believe we should adopt Sara Bareilles' song, "Brave", as internal audit's professional anthem.)

Most CAEs who bring bad news and run afoul of the CEO or CFO leave their company within the next nine months.

When I had my moment in the spotlight and told the audit committee that there was a culture issue they needed to know, I took the steps I thought critical but missed one. The result was not a good one.

The team had uncovered accounting frauds, primarily in the US but also in Asia. In the US, general managers and their controllers had inflated their earnings, generally using concocted journal entries. (We found this at multiple sites, but there was no evidence either that managers of one site conspired with another, or even that they knew what the other was doing.)

The managers did this so that they could achieve their financial targets; if they failed to do so, they believed there was a high risk their site would be closed down.

In Asia, for a number of years financial management had used "cookie jar" accounting to manipulate earnings (they put profits in a reserve or provision account when times were good and withdrew them when needed to improve profits).

Their motivation was different than in the US: they were highly profitable, but wanted to inflate their earnings to make up for shortfalls in other parts of the world.

Unfortunately, all of the financial managers involved said they felt encouraged to "make the number" by the finance leadership in corporate.

There was absolutely no evidence that any of the corporate finance leaders ever encouraged them to make their numbers through inappropriate accounting.

Certainly there was pressure to perform and achieve targets, but we didn't find anything to indicate that corporate told site managers to do what they did.

At the same time, it was clear (at least to me) that corporate finance had not done enough to stress the importance of financial integrity and responsibility to finance professionals across the organization.

The audit committee knew about the investigations and the frauds. I had included that information in my regular reports, and when necessary had conversations between audit committee meetings with the chairman of the committee.

Fortunately, none of the frauds had been individually or in aggregate material to the financial results of the company as a whole. However, I believed the audit committee needed to know the root cause of the frauds – a culture that seemed to encourage "making the numbers" without stressing the need to do so through performance rather than fiction.

I knew that this was not going to be an easy task for me.

It was complicated because I didn't report with a solid line to the audit committee. After I joined the company, a new CFO arrived and changed my direct reporting line from the audit committee to him (without objection from the board). While he allowed me full access to the committee, I knew he was not happy with my independent spirit.

My first step was to talk to other CAEs I respected and to people at the IIA. They were supportive but only confirmed what I already knew: I had an obligation to tell the audit committee, it was not going to be easy, and this was the kind of situation where the CAE may be shot as the messenger of unwelcome news.

So I sat down with the CFO. He listened attentively and did not argue when I said I felt obligated to report to the audit committee.

Without him asking, I volunteered that I would tell the audit committee that I had no reason to believe that anybody in corporate finance, including him, had deliberately created this environment. But, I felt that the appropriate action would be for him to issue a message that reinforced the expectation that everybody involved in finance take ownership for the integrity of the numbers they reported.

He agreed that I would start the briefing to the committee. He would then add his comments, confirming that to the best of his knowledge nobody in corporate finance had encouraged or even known about the inappropriate accounting, and that he would communicate his expectations as I had suggested.

I said that we needed to inform the CEO so he wouldn't be surprised by my report to the audit committee (he generally attended the meetings). I asked that the two of us meet with the CEO and brief him.

To my surprise and dismay, the CEO not only said he would take care of the CEO but forbade me (with a severe look) from talking to the CEO.

I told the CFO I would talk to the chair of the audit committee, to which he agreed.

My conversation with the chair of the audit committee went very well.

He listened and asked the right questions. He agreed with the plan that I speak and then the CFO add a few words.

He said that he would comment as well, confirming his agreement that the recommended communication by the CFO should be sufficient at this point and that the audit committee should support my continuing focus on the integrity of financial reporting at these and similar locations.

I asked the chair if I should have separate conversations with the other two members of the audit committee. He said it was not necessary. They were both strong supporters of mine and he said he would find a way to talk to them informally and in person ahead of the meeting. (The audit committee normally met on the second or third day of board meetings.)

On the day of the meeting, the CFO and I were alone in the board room for a few minutes. He asked me if I was ready and I said I was.

I thought I was as I knew all of the audit committee members appreciated my work, had always been exceptionally friendly, and both in meetings and in one-on-one conversations had demonstrated their trust in me. After all, I had been working with audit committees for about a dozen years by then.

I started my presentation by reminding the audit committee that we had found a number of accounting frauds. None were material, but we were concerned about why there had been so many in the last year. I explained that I interviewed each of the responsible finance controllers to see if I could understand what had motivated them.

I told the audit committee that the common thread was a message from corporate finance (not always the same person) that they needed to make their number.

None of the controllers said they had been told to "make up" the numbers, but they all felt the pressure. I talked about the COSO Control Environment component and the idea of "tone at the top".

I said that I had spoken to the individuals in corporate finance whom the controllers had been talking to, but there was no indication that they had wanted the financial controllers to do more than work with site management to improve the results for the quarter, for example by offering additional discounts to accelerate sales.

No sooner had I said that there was no evidence that the CFO or any of his direct reports either knew about the frauds or were any way involved than one of the audit committee members started yelling. He was yelling at me.

The yelling director had been my most ardent supporter. For example, he had asked me to attend the IT committee meetings, which he chaired, because (he told me) he valued highly my insights and advice.

Now he was yelling at me. He challenged my saying that I had no reason to believe anybody in corporate was involved. He screamed, with a face to match, that he didn't believe me; I was hiding something from him and the other committee members.

I admit it: I was in shock.

My face was as white as his was red.

I repeated that I had no reason to believe corporate was involved. I was not hiding anything. I was not colluding with the CFO or anybody else.

I looked around for support.

The CFO was sitting back in his chair. Quiet. Calm. Not coming to my support and looking as if he was not even thinking of it. He looked neither surprised nor disappointed.

The audit committee chairman was leaning forward, looking worried. He didn't say anything for what seemed like an eternity.

When he spoke, it was to calm the board member down rather than voice support for me. The third board member added his voice of reason.

Eventually, the presentation and the audit committee meeting were over.

But not before I had lost my trust in the CFO, much of my credibility with the screaming board member, and some of my confidence that the audit committee chairman would support me when management did not – even when he agreed with what I was doing and saying.

By the way, the external auditors were present and they also knew what I was going to report. They didn't say anything in the meeting, but I didn't expect them to and don't blame them for their silence.

I survived but the CFO felt little to no pressure to say anything about integrity in accounting.

I left the company within the year – and was happy to do so!

∞

If I were to do this all over again, I would have taken one more important step.

There was nothing I could do about my reporting relationship. For whatever reason, the audit committee had not stood up to the CFO and insisted that I report directly to them. I could also not have done anything about the refusal of the CFO to let me brief the CEO.

But what I should have done is brief each of the audit committee members, preferably with the audit committee chairman on the call, before the meeting.

If I had done that, I would have found out what the chairman told me when I called him after the meeting.

The irate director had been on the board of another company where there had been financial statement fraud and the CFO had been involved. When I started talking about "making the numbers", all he could think of was what had happened at his last company. He knew that I reported to the CFO and was afraid that had influenced me.

It didn't make sense. I would not have even raised the issue if I had been colluding with the CFO, but he was not thinking rationally.

I should have ensured that each of the committee members, the CEO and CFO, and the audit partners not only knew what I was going to say, but had asked all their questions and voiced their concerns before the meeting. If they had been briefed in a less formal setting, with nobody watching how they reacted, the audit committee meeting itself would have been a smoothly orchestrated and successful event.

As you can imagine, those few minutes when I was confronted by a screaming friend (or so I had thought of him until that moment, when he became a screaming fiend) will live with me forever.

An epitaph is suitable. Within a few years of my leaving, the company admitted failure and allowed itself to be acquired by its strongest competitor. Its culture problems went beyond financial reporting; internal division and infighting among the executives led to the loss of customers and revenue, an inability to rationalize operations, and the death of the company.

Chapter 35: The expansion of internal auditing

About a year after I started at Tosco, the director responsible for vendor contracts in our Avon refinery (in Northern California) came to me with an interesting proposition. He had the support of his manager, the Vice President and Controller for that part of our business (Tosco Refining Company, or TRC).

The proposition was that internal audit should perform audits of the refinery's main vendors.

The director assured me that it was a win-win proposition. This kind of auditing always brought in (over a period) far more in terms of recoveries from vendor over-billings than it cost. He had worked at organizations where the return on the investment was as much as 500%.

The TRC Controller supported not only internal auditing performing these audits, but increasing my budget so I could add resources and not impair my ability to perform traditional internal auditing.

I talked to some experts in contracts auditing who confirmed what the director said. I thought about engaging one or more consulting firms as there were a few specializing in our industry (oil refining). R.L Townsend and Associates was perhaps the most highly-respected, but they were very busy. Instead, they suggested I consider hiring Bill Baker.

With the blessing of HR, I interviewed Bill Baker and was incredibly impressed. He is a true genius in this area, with extensive experience not only as an auditor but as a general contractor. Bill had performed construction and contracts audits around the world for several oil companies, delivering millions in savings.

I hired Bill with the understanding that he had to demonstrate a positive ROI within the year. In hindsight, I severely underestimated him.

Bill found all kind of issues with contract billings. Some were straightforward overcharges according to the contract. Others were more sophisticated, even amusing in hindsight.

For example, one of the contracts where he audited vendor billings related to "refractory services". Every few years, parts of our refinery were taken out of service for maintenance (what is referred to as a "turnaround"). Because we essentially boiled crude oil in the refinery, a layer of material would build up on the walls of some of the units. This had to be removed and, where necessary, the coating of the units replaced.

The Avon refinery routinely hired a specialist company (usually the same one each time) to do the refractory work during turnarounds. Bill audited their billings, which were under a time and material contract. The vendor was to bill us at agreed labor rates for each category of employee; different rates were established for different levels of experience, from master to trainee.

However, Bill found that the vendor was billing everybody at "master" rates!

He met with the owner of the company and asked him about this. The vendor said that the billings were correct! Bill asked how that could be. He had looked at the employees' backgrounds and while some clearly merited the "master" title, some had no related experience. They were trainees and should have been billed at that rate, at least for the first year.

Bill estimated the overcharges at around $600,000 (a lot of money in 1991).

The vendor stuck to his grounds. He asserted that _he_ was the person who determined whether an individual was a master or a trainee and he had decided they were all masters. Nothing in the contract prevented him doing that.

Bill and I met with management, who were understandably shocked. Although the manager in charge of refinery maintenance was concerned that we not damage relations with the vendor, his manager pressed him to negotiate aggressively.

We not only obtained a full refund, but the vendor changed his practices (we continued dealing with him as his firm was the best available option in our area) and Bill proved his immense value to the corporation.

In the first year, Bill's work delivered an ROI of about 1000%. In other words, as a result of his audits, management was able to negotiate and recover overcharges that were about 10 times what the audits cost.

Management was keen for me to expand the contracts auditing function. I was able to hire an outstanding, experienced and talented leader for the new function in Connie Chapman. Over the years, with her leadership, we built the team up to about 28 people (as many as I had in the traditional internal audit side) and they consistently had an ROI of between 10 and 12 times cost.

∞

One year, Connie and her team audited the largest vendor of our marketing business (Tosco Marketing Company, or TMC, headquartered in Phoenix, Arizona). Management and the vendor settled the negotiation of the overcharges we reported with a combination of a credit to our account of about $6 million and a reduction in charges going forward.

Later that year, I attended the TMC executive off-site meeting. The purpose was to review the nearly-completed year and agree on plans for the upcoming year.

The TMC CFO led the opening session with a review of the financial results for the almost-completed year. The first slide was a summary of actual vs. budget.

Somebody noticed that the CFO had a line item, below the pre-tax profit line, with "audit results". When asked, he said that this represented the contribution of my contracts audit team. He had put it 'below the line' because it "distorted the financial results for the year".

We then spent about an hour talking about whether the CFO should project similar savings in the new year.

∞

On the East Coast, we had a similarly strong contracts audit team, led by Matt Melone. Not only did Matt bring experience, insight, and results, but he initiated a maturing of our contracts audit work.

With his leadership, we moved from after-the-fact recovery of vendor overcharges and identification of poor contracting that led to costs exceeding our intention, to a more proactive approach.

Matt established such a positive relationship with management of our East Coast operations that they asked him to consult on contract structure.

One of our problems was that when we audited a contract, we found not only overcharges but loopholes that the vendor had exploited. Frequently, we were only able to negotiate the recovery of a portion of the overcharges and help management fix the contract going forward – and we had lost the time value of the funds involved.

Matt started performing "pre-audits" before a contract was negotiated. (This was also being done on the West Coast, but I think Matt perfected the idea.) He was able to help refinery management negotiate better contracts, not only more favorable in terms of pricing but also minimizing vendor overcharges.

∞

The President of our Refining Company, Dwight Wiggins, loved the work we did. He commented to me that when he toured a refinery during a turnaround he looked for the white hats worn by my auditors. I asked him whether he liked to see that because he could see we were on site and working with the vendors.

> "No, Norman. I like to see the white hats because I know the contractors can see them and know they are being watched! It's a great deterrent against fraud."

The contracts audit team represented about half of my team at Tosco. But, I had two other groups that were not performing traditional audits.

∞

The first is one that is often within the internal audit remit: investigations.

Until Tosco acquired the Circle K convenience store business, investigations were handled by a combination of HR (for suspected violation of HR-related policies – the most common occurrence); Environment, Health, and Safety (for issues related to their compliance responsibilities); Security (for routine theft and damage to property); and, internal audit. Now that we had a convenience store business, we needed a team of specialists to investigate suspected fraud and so on.

Over the years, I had not only received training in fraud investigations, but had performed a few investigations myself. I knew that should the investigation be performed ineptly, a risk to the organization far greater than any loss might be created.

In addition to the principles I discussed in Chapter 25, experience has shown me that:

1. Investigations should only be performed by individuals who have been sufficiently trained and experienced. When I formed a team at Tosco, one of the requirements was that the investigators hold a Certified Fraud Examiner (CFE) credential and had demonstrated, to my satisfaction, their abilities by performing investigations under the direct supervision of a CFE

2. The determination of whether a fraud has been committed is a legal responsibility. The investigator reports the facts, an attorney determines whether there has been a violation of the code of conduct and/or law, and management determines any disciplinary action
3. Although evidence will often build during an investigation that points to the "guilt" of an individual or group, investigators should not allow themselves to start to believe in that guilt until all the evidence is in. Very often, the "suspect" is not interviewed until late in the investigation so there is always a possibility that when he is interviewed additional evidence that points to innocence will be found. For example, I have seen and performed investigations where an individual did something that violated the code, only to find when he was interviewed that he did it at the express direction of his manager

∞

I could write many pages about all the frauds that we uncovered, but I will share just one, my favorite.

Marty Patton was auditing a small subsidiary and found a curious journal entry. If I recall correctly, the journal entry consisted of a debit to the bonus accrual (or similar) and a credit to revenue. It was a very strange entry. He was looking at the piece of paper it was written on when he noticed some writing on the back. It was a calculation:

Target	x
Projected Actual	(y)
Difference	z

"Difference" was the amount credited to revenue!

Marty sat down with the general ledger accountant and her supervisor. He asked if they could explain the journal entry as he didn't understand it.

They replied that they had not written it. He asked who did, and they said it was the subsidiary's controller. Then he asked whether they had seen this type of journal before, to which they replied:

> "You mean the Main Street journal entries?"

> "Why Main Street?"

> "Because that's the address of the county courthouse!"

∞

Years later, at Business Objects, management asked that I start a group to audit our customers' compliance with the licensing terms of our contracts.

Like many if not most software companies, we had a lot of revenue "leakage" as companies extended their use of our software beyond what was permitted by the license. Under the charismatic leadership of Steve Wozniak (not the Apple co-founder), the license compliance team brought in millions in additional revenue to the company.

∞

There was one other group that I picked up at Tosco.

The head of IT operations (Bill) asked to meet with me and asked me to do him a favor. Bill told me that consultants had advised him to start a Quality Assurance group. It was charged with ensuring all new applications and changes to existing applications were developed according to company policy and properly tested. I thought that was a great idea, one I knew my IT audit group supported.

Apparently, the consultants had suggested that IT outsource the function to them, as it was one of their areas of excellence. Bob had tried that but was very unhappy with the results, so he hired a QA manager and brought it all in-house. Now he had decided that managing QA from within IT wasn't going to work either.

Could I take on QA in addition to Internal Audit? He said that I had a reputation for excellence as a manager and leader (flattery will get you everywhere) and thought that I would be successful taking QA where it needed to go.

I asked him about whether I could consider QA as an independent function (of IT management) and he agreed that would be a key to its success. I realized that there would be some level of synergy with the IA audit team, so I agreed to take it on and Bill transferred the budget and staff.

There were only two people in QA. Each was outstanding, so it didn't take much for me to help them stay on track. In fact, the toughest part of managing QA was helping them establish and then maintain a constructive working relationship with IT.

Apparently, the positive relationship and reputation that people like Tim Cox, Bruce Taylor, Will Helton, Don Villa, and Alan Proctor (my IT audit team) had with IT management and staff was the key to get QA past the problems of their past.

I took on QA for these reasons:

1. It would not impair either my independence and objectivity as CAE
2. It would not impair my ability to provide the assurance and advisory services that I considered essential
3. It was the right thing to do for the company as a whole
4. The audit committee gave their formal approval, based on it all of the above

I am always open to taking on other responsibilities when I can satisfy those four requirements.

Over the years, I also stepped up at management request to take on the responsibilities of being the Chief Compliance Officer (including Ethics) and Chief Risk Officer.

Chapter 36: World-class internal auditing

What is world-class? In the Introduction, I said that "world-class" is something that is only achieved when customers, peer organizations, and so on refer to you as world-class.

My team has been recognized by our primary stakeholders on the audit committee and in executive management for excellence.

We were honored to be selected by Bob Hirth to be the first internal audit department to be profiled by Arthur Andersen in their *KnowledgeSpace* best practices service (which became Protiviti's *KnowledgeLeader*).

The team and I were also profiled in a *Journal of Accountancy* article in November 1998 (the magazine of the American Institute of Public Accountants), and I was identified as an innovative internal audit leader by an IIA publication in 1997.

World-class does not mean that your internal audit organization meets the standards for best-in-class departments as defined by a consultant. When consulting firms issue these reports on best practices among internal audit departments, they are basing their comments on what their surveys say companies are doing plus their own opinions on what is best practice.

What is reported as "best practice" is either what has worked for other companies or what the consultant writing the report thinks is a good idea.

But, a world-class organization is trying out techniques that few are aware of, let alone adopting. They won't show up in surveys.

Instead, "best practice" and "world-class" should refer to what is best for your company at this time.

For example, VMWare is a technology company based in Northern California. Their CAE, Susan Insley, understands that the organization is in the midst of continued, radical change. It is setting up new departments and bringing new products to market all the time.

Rather than performing traditional point-in-time audits, she has staffed her team with individuals who not only have internal audit but risk management skills and experience. Her audit engagements are focused on helping management understand the risks they face as they embark on these new ventures.

She "audits forward".

This is world-class because she has adapted to meet the needs of the organization. As the organization matures, she will likely adapt again.

Chris Keller has been the CAE at Apple, also based on Northern California, for about 18 years. He is always looking for ways to optimize the value that internal audit brings to the organization.

With audit committee and executive management support, he (like Susan) performs few traditional point-in-time audits.

His team are "embedded" in all major initiatives, monitoring the quality of controls and ensuring that management is not only managing risks but continuously assessing and communicating the level of risks they are taking to senior management.

I have great respect for the way he is "auditing forward" and being very proactive. He is also quick to eliminate audit activities (such as audit working papers) that have little value.

Throughout my career, like Susan and Chris, I have tried to modify our audit plan and strategy to what the company needed most.

Sometimes, like at the start of my times with Tosco and Maxtor, we needed to focus on basic, core business processes because they were not mature. But, as they matured I moved my audit plan to where the risks were and were going to be, auditing forward and proactively.

Both strategies need the type of people who can execute on them. People who are not satisfied with routine "inspect and verify" auditing, but are keen to help the organization grow and succeed.

∞

Rick Teubner was an audit manager of this ilk in my Northern California team (led by Roger Herd) at Tosco. This is what he has to say:

> "You demonstrated to Executive Management that IA is adding value in excess of costs, which ensures the function is well-funded. Even though we were in an environment where budgets were highly scrutinized, we had the resources to do our work properly and budgets didn't negatively impacted employee retention or morale. An effective leader supports the team with appropriate resources.
>
> "Your audit team had the appropriate level of expertise and knowledge to execute their audits. Some IA functions are tempted to primarily hire junior staff, following the model used by most CPA firms; however, it's difficult for inexperienced auditors to work effectively with auditees. An effective leader doesn't expect the groups being audited to train the audit team.
>
> "Having geographically based audit teams, with you traveling to the locations regularly, ensured that each location had a continual audit presence. When auditors travel to outlying locations periodically, rather than having a home base in the region, some parts of the organization won't get the attention that they need and the audit presence is limited. An effective leader views all operations as being within their sphere of influence, regardless of distance to the location or travel preferences.
>
> "Your audit plans are based on the appropriate risks to the organization, based on industry knowledge and feedback from the operational leaders. It's easy to develop an audit plan that attempts to cover everything end-to-end, but these plans ultimately result in limited coverage as auditors scramble to touch on each area of operations without providing in-depth coverage

of any risks. An effective leader addresses the important risks with the appropriate level of coverage and doesn't waste time on immaterial activities.

"Your audit results are presented in a manner that helps an organization improve their business, rather than the zero-sum game that many audit organizations fall into of auditors attempting to make themselves look good by making someone else look bad. When an audit function becomes adversarial, audits become more difficult to execute and all recommendations are dead on arrival, which reinforces why you put effort into having a good relationships with your auditees. An effective leader doesn't have to rely on making others look bad in order to show the value that they add to the organization.

"You encourage auditors to be concerned about their image, and to avoid the typical stereotypes that give many auditors a bad reputation. Simply put, it's hard to be effective if people don't enjoy working with the audit team. An effective leader creates a brand image for their audit department and reinforces the need to create the right impression."

∞

I have presented several times around the world on the topic of "My ideal internal audit department". Here are its 18 attributes:

1. **Praised by the audit committee and top management because they "help them sleep at night."**

As I mentioned earlier, I believe the primary mission for internal audit is to provide the audit committee and top management with the assurance they need as they direct and manage the organization.

They need to know not only that value is protected, but that the enterprise has the people, processes, systems, and organization (including controls) to seize opportunities.

They need to know that the organization will be able to execute on strategies and plans and achieve or exceed its objectives.

This means that the internal audit team must focus on the risks that matter to the organization, including the risks that are emerging and will be important to future success.

It also means that the CAE must communicate assurance, not just provide traditional audit reports with a list of findings.

There should be a formal report to the audit committee and top management with an opinion on the adequacy of the organization's ability to manage the more significant risks to its objectives at acceptable levels.

Those risks can exceed acceptable levels due to failures in business processes; the identification, assessment, evaluation, and management of risk; and in governance. All of these should be considered and addressed as appropriate in the audit plan – which is updated dynamically as risks change.

The ISO 31000:2009 global risk management standard has a number of principles. One of which is that effective risk management is "dynamic, iterative, and responsive to change".

Internal audit should likewise have a plan that is dynamic, iterative, and responsive to change.

2. **A cool place to work.**

How do you get the most out of people? Let them feel enriched, valued, and able to make a difference.

There's a reason that Silicon Valley firms let their people play while they are working – because when people enjoy their work they are innovative, imaginative, and deliver results.

There is no reason that internal auditors can't enjoy their work and obtain both personal and personal gratification.

I am pleased, flattered, and sad when I meet and break bread with my former colleagues. They always remark on how much they enjoyed being part of the great team we had. They remark that I was one of the best managers they have had (and sometimes ask me to start my own company so they can join it). But more to the point, they miss each other and the team spirit they enjoyed.

3. **The department people want to transfer to, but hate to leave.**

There have been several times when I have to push people to leave internal audit. I guess that's the downside of their having so much fun, but for the sake of their careers I have not just found positions for my people (within the company) but had extended arguments with them to get them to move.

I am a strong believer that the best auditors are those who have walked in the other person's shoes. In this case, I am talking about the shoes of the operating management.

I don't believe I would have had the success and recognition that I have been lucky to receive if I hadn't spent several years in line management.

I know what it is to make my number, to meet a budget, and to be audited. I know how frustrating it can be to have an auditor take your to-do list and turn it into his list of findings. I also know what it is like to have an auditor list actions that he knows I don't have the resources to perform, but refuses to say anything about the lack of resources.

If we are to communicate effectively, we need to know and use the language of the business. That comes most easily when you have lived in that foreign land.

If we are to make business-practical recommendations for improvement, it is essential to understand the business, including the realities of resource constraints and politics.

I believe the best CAEs are those who have a combination of public accounting, internal auditing, and line management experience.

4. **Where people think!**

How can an internal auditor add value by coming up with new ideas and recommended actions to improve the business, when management and staff in the business have been focused on that business process for years?

It's not by following a checklist or from reading a book.

It may be from seeing a similar situation in another environment (another location within the business or at another company) and understanding how practices there might apply to the current situation.

(Soon after I started the internal audit group at Tosco, the Tosco newsletter editor asked me for an interview so she could profile internal audit, I spoke to her and then asked that she talk to my team: Debra Davies, Laura Nathlich, Michael Brooding, and Lorie Reynolds. Debra told her that one of the values of internal audit to an organization is that we are like butterflies, flitting from one flower to the next, spreading best practices and ideas.)

New ideas and suggestions for improving business processes and practices come from people who can think.

Yes, they may have seen something before, but they have to know how to apply it to the specific situation. What may be "best practice" for one organization may not be for the next. The organization may be structured differently, they may use different systems, the risks may at different levels, and the culture and style of the organization may be different.

I like to think that internal auditors can be imaginative, creative, and resourceful. I love it when an auditor (such as Soo Wai Mun in Singapore at Solectron) would literally sit down with a unit controller and together they work out the best solution to a problem. Wai Mun built a relationship with this controller who frequently called her to discuss issues totally unrelated to the audit Wai Mun had led.

CAEs need to force their team members to use their often-forgotten imaginations. There is truth to the notion that we are far more creative as children than as adults. That is especially so when we are trained not to think for ourselves but do what we are told as junior auditors.

I am afraid that most of the people I have interviewed who have spent most of the career in public accounting have been taught not to think. They are told follow directions, stick to the audit program, and don't challenge authority. Frequently, they are not taught the fundamentals of the topic they are auditing. For example, few have read and studied Auditing Standard Number 5, even though it dictates the top-down and risk-based approach they should be using to assess internal control over financial reporting.

I try not to give my team answers when they come to me with questions. I challenge and try to stretch them to find the answers themselves.

I hate standard audit programs and checklists. These are crutches for auditors who don't want to think. The programs and checklists publicly available on the web worked for one company but may not be right for yours.

The audit programs from the last audit of the area at the same company were from a time when the risks were probably different, the staff and even the processes may have changed. While they can be useful reminders of things to consider, every audit program should be considered a new task.

Mike Wilmouth worked for me first, as a Contracts Audit Manager, first at Tosco and then at Solectron. This is what he has to say:

> "I was on one of my first contract audit assignments and approached Norman to determine if a standard audit template existed by which to cover specified basic elements to ensure quality expectations were met. Norman's response was that no such template existed except in my mind and it was up to my imagination and experience to make the determination as to the project scope.
>
> "Norman has promoted in my life and career an "out of the box" approach to analyzing any life situation no matter whether in a personal or professional setting.
>
> "The norms of any of our professions are continuously being challenged by "out of the box" thinkers that are both personally and professionally rewarded in ways that the normal aspects of our jobs will never offer."

When assessing what look like deficiencies in controls or risk management, auditors need to think. Does this really represent a risk that is at an unacceptable level for the organization? How can it best be brought within acceptable levels, given cost and resource constraints? What is the root cause? What would I do if I owned the business?

Paper after paper talk about the new software and technologies available to improve the professional practice of internal auditing.

In my opinion, the most underutilized tools and the ones most likely to bring immense value are:

- The auditor's ears: so they can listen to what people have to say
- The auditor's eyes: so they can not only see issues and their indicators (such as a messy warehouse) but pick up the 80% of communication that is non-verbal, and

- The space in between: so they can think about what they hear and see. They can make accurate assessments and make valuable suggestions for improvement

5. **Where people are set free to choose an audit approach that stimulates and develops, as well as getting to the heart of the problem — tackling the root issues head on.**

There are more than a hundred ways to perform an audit. I know, I once put together a mind map (Figure 7, below) that attempts to capture at least some of them. If I were to update the mind map, I could probably add quite a few more with all the new technology and other ideas available.

Figure 7: Audit Choices

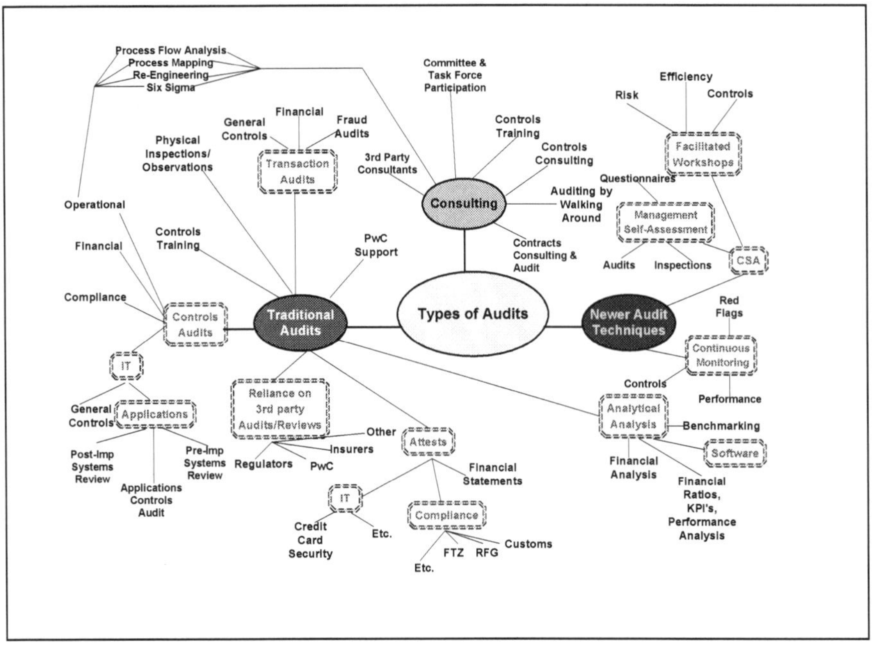

I like to agree with the auditor who leads the project on its scope and end-product (typically assurance on one or more risk areas). Then I let the auditor determine *how* they will perform the audit.

They might opt for one of the techniques included in the mind map, or they might come up with something that is new to me. Perhaps they have seen a novel use of technology and I am always keen to hear about such innovations.

For example, my friend Mark Gosling (currently CAE at NetApp, but at that time CAE of Verisign) told me about an interesting use of gamification software.

A simulated stock exchange is set up and the only stock is the project you want to monitor. It might be an IT implementation or any other initiative. Everybody involved in the project, including the project manager and his team, the business users, other affected departments, and consultants can participate by buying or selling shares in the project. When there is general optimism that the project will succeed, people will want to buy and the price goes up. When prospects dim, the price falls. By monitoring changes in the price of the stock, auditors can monitor the true feelings of those involved and whether they believe the project will succeed or not. If and when it drops, auditors can interview participants to find out whether issues have been identified but not reported to project management and to them.

When there is an issue, it is critical that the auditor get to the root cause.

Very often, that root cause is people.

It may be that there is too much work for the people to be able to handle; I don't know why, but internal auditors seem very reluctant to include this as a relevant fact in their audit report. The root cause may also be poor management.

I learned this the hard way with a situation that (in hindsight) was at times comical and ended up as a tragedy.

I was visiting my team and management of a major business unit in the US when I heard that the unit's CEO was running around the building, angry and anxious. Apparently, one of our accounting groups had processed an invoice against the counterparty to a derivatives trade that was not only wrong but absurdly wrong.

The company was a very active user of derivatives transactions to hedge the prices of its raw materials and finished products. On occasion, it entered into "swap" trades with counterparties in the business or with financial institutions. In these trades, one company would agree to purchase quantities of one product and sell quantities of another to the other party at a certain date. Initially, the value of each of the two transactions would be the same. The market prices would fluctuate and when the agreed date arrived, one party would owe the other a (typically) small amount – the difference between the value from the sale and the cost of the purchase. However, on this occasion our accounting group sent the counterparty an invoice for the full amount of the sale side of the swap, not the difference.

Our CEO was running around looking for a two *billion* dollar invoice! He ran from accounting to IT to the room with the printers to the mail room. Eventually it was found, fortunately before it was mailed to the counterparty and our reputation damaged.

We had an audit scheduled for that accounting group and it was clear that we needed to move it up in the schedule. The audit team understood that we needed to understand what happened and get to the root cause so it would never happen again.

The team found a lot of issues, including the fact that the accountants were not sufficiently familiar with what the traders were doing. This led to our recommendation to have them sit in the same room.

When we asked the manager of the accounting group why his team had made an error, he said it was because HR would not give him the budget to hire people with a CPA. He was forced to get the job done with people who not only didn't have a CPA but may not have gone to college. This put an immense burden on him, because he had to insert himself into every activity. He was overloaded, tired, and mistakes will happen.

My team told me this and I asked them what they thought about the staff this manager had working for him. Were they as inept as he said?

Absolutely not, they insisted. Although they didn't have the CPA certification, they had many years of experience in this type of accounting and a deep understanding of the business – deeper than the manager!

I had known this manager for several years and knew he was bright, immensely hard-working and dedicated, and considered a top performer by senior management.

My team went back and asked a few more questions. The staff told them that they didn't believe the manager trusted them. He gave them tasks but never explained why he wanted something done. So they never really knew whether what they had done was right. The manager kept all information about the business and its activities to himself; they did the best they could, but morale was low and they were all looking for other jobs.

The manager confirmed what they had said. He didn't trust them beyond performing tasks to his detailed instructions. He kept all decisions to himself because he was the only CPA, the only one qualified and trained to make the decisions.

This was tough. It was clear to me that the manager was the problem. He was an abysmal leader and wasted the talents of his staff. He either had to change or go.

I met with the CFO and then the CEO of the business unit. They decided to let the manager go.

He had been somebody I considered a friend, somebody I respected. But he had been promoted beyond his management capabilities.

A new manager was appointed and soon the accounting group was back on an even keel.

The audit report we issued after the audit was completed didn't detail what we found. That was addressed directly in meetings with management and the audit committee. I find that is usually the best way to communicate sensitive issues.

When we limit our communication of audit results to the formal audit report, we limit ourselves. In this case, the audit report included a comment that I would discuss the matter further with senior management and the audit committee. But what I had to say to them was entirely in person, verbal, and not written down.

If I needed to communicate to senior management that the bank or account reconciliations were not being done because there weren't enough people, I might mention a resource issue in the audit report but discuss the root cause, the decision to cut headcount without consideration of its effect, in a less confrontational manner.

After all, our job is not to score points telling people how many mistakes they have made. Our job is to help people understand whether things are OK and, when they are not, work with them to effect the necessary change.

6. **The source of projects that are noticed, that will be told to the team's grandchildren.**

Over the years, my teams have completed audit engagements and other activities that are worthy of sharing with our grandchildren (Tom Peters' definition of a Wow! project). I am not talking about finding frauds. I am talking about work we have done that made a huge difference to the business. They include:

- The Business Objects license compliance team making enough money through their audits to let the company meet its EPS targets for the year
- The Tosco contracts auditing team making so much money for the Marketing company that the CFO had to put their recoveries on a separate line "because they distorted the results for the year"

- The IT audit team at Tosco identifying all the points where the new store system would fail, enabling management to be prepared and to respond when those failures occurred – minimizing any damage
- The Maxtor team helping the company go from multiple material weaknesses to not even a significant deficiency, in just one year
- The Business Objects team persuading the external auditor, through the quality of their work, to rely on them for 80% of the testing (a number provided by the audit partner) and cut one million dollars from the audit fee
- Loretta's Wow! project (see Chapter 27)

When internal audit focuses on the risks that matter to the organization, provides objective and insightful assurance on how well they are managed, and use their intellect and imagination to work with management to effect necessary changes, amazing things can and do happen.

7. **The internal consultants of choice and a source of talent.**

Why should management go to an outside consulting firm when they have an internal audit team that understands the business, is composed of quality individuals with experience and insight, and is committed to helping the organization succeed?

There are times when special skills or insights are needed that internal audit does not possess. But many of the projects given to the consulting arms of the accounting firms might have been given to internal audit at a fraction of the cost – and probably with better results.

There are also times when internal audit doesn't have the bandwidth to take on additional projects without impairing its responsibilities to provide assurance on the risks that matter.

Yet, a sign of a world-class internal audit department is that the CAE's phone is always ringing.

I once had a period when my IT audit team in Phoenix was turning over at annualized rate of 400%!

I was not worried about it. I was proud of it!

No sooner had I hired a new IT audit team member (they were all at manager level or better) and exposed them to management than IT offered them jobs. Soon the entire IT security team was managed and staffed by people I had hired for internal audit, led by Dick Leonard and Richard Busch.

I am proud that so many of my team has gone on to executive positions (including as CAE). While some CAEs prohibit anybody leaving to join a business unit until they have served two years. I don't take that position. When the company as a whole and the employee both benefit from the move, I will support it.

However, I frown on the idea that people are hired for their potential after they leave internal audit. I also don't like the idea of a rotation of people through internal audit who are not competent to perform quality audit work. I am totally opposed to making a top performer CAE for a period (e.g., out of marketing or finance) when he or she is unlikely to provide the leadership necessary to make internal audit world-class.

When people are motivated by their career outside internal audit, they are at best conflicted and at worst unable to be objective.

8. **At the exit interview, the manager says (sincerely) thank you.**

Customer surveys paint a picture, but it is questionable how real and reliable that picture is.

When an audit identifies a lot of issues, the survey is unlikely to be glowing. When a survey comes back glowing, it could simply be because the audit found little and so caused minimal trouble for management.

I believe the best feedback from an audit is what you hear from your customers (both operational and senior management, and the audit committee) and what you see in their eyes when they provide feedback in person. We all know how to distinguish honest from false notes of appreciation.

The way that management works with the internal auditor prior to, during, and following the close meeting speaks volumes.

Even more is said when, as CAE, I meet with management at all levels and ask if we are adding value to their organization. I don't want to hear that we are "OK", as that usually means they are putting up with us rather than seeing us as adding value. I prefer to hear that our audit at least confirmed, through our opinion, that everything is working the way they want. Even better is when they say that our insights will help them improve.

Better yet are comments (which I have received and mentioned earlier):

- "You haven't done an audit I wouldn't gladly pay for"
- "I won't go forward with an major systems implementation ever again without first obtaining the insights from your IT audit team"
- "Can you help us figure out how we can make the necessary changes?"
- "Can I hire your auditor?"

Are we really adding value if our customer doesn't say, with appreciation, that we are helping them and the organization succeed? Its to be treasured when they say that when you are not present.

9. **Fully leverages the organization's risk management processes (automated processes, by the way).**

If the organization's risk management processes are sufficiently mature, internal audit should place as much reliance as possible on their identification, assessment, evaluation, and monitoring of risks. Internal audit should adapt the enterprise risk reporting rather than seek to duplicate it.

For example, Andrew MacLeod is the CAE at the Brisbane City Council in Australia. He works closely with his organization's risk management team.

When it is time to update his audit plan, Andrew takes the enterprise assessment for each risk and modifies it based on a number of factors, such as the number and level of issues found in the prior audit; whether there has been significant change in people, processes, or systems; and so on. These factors represent the level of confidence he has that the controls management relies upon to manage that risk are operating effectively as designed. The end product is an audit-adjusted risk universe on which he will base his audit plan.

Before internal audit can place reliance on the enterprise risk management program, it has to audit it. I think the IIA has done a good job providing guidance in its *Practice Guide: Reliance by Internal Audit on Other Assurance Providers.*

If the risk management program is not sufficiently mature, the CAE must ensure that the audit committee and top management understand the facts and what they mean.

For most organizations, the greatest risk is that they don't know what the risks are! They make decisions, set strategy, and monitor performance without appropriate consideration of risk and uncertainty, and without taking the actions necessary and appropriate to optimize results.

In these situations, internal audit should become an evangelist for risk management. It should help management at all levels understand what they are missing and how to address it. It should also work with the risk management team as both their cheerleader and mentor, as appropriate.

I do not believe that internal audit should assume responsibility for risk assessment and taking actions to manage risk. These remain a management responsibility. Internal audit can lead the risk management function as long as management retains ownership and responsibility for risk assessment and decisions about what risks to take, how to manage them, and so on. I like the IIA's Position Paper: *The Role of Internal Auditing in Enterprise-wide Risk Management*.

10. **Fully leverages advanced continuous monitoring and auditing capabilities – as part of a risk-based audit program.**

While internal audit can be world-class without relying heavily technology tools, my ideal internal audit department will:

- Provide every auditor not only with a laptop, but with a tablet
- Enable every auditor to use analytics, including mobile analytics, to obtain the information necessary to be effective – in understanding the business and its trends, automated testing, and monitoring risks
- Always be looking at how technology can make internal audit more effective and more efficient. It is not sufficient to understand enough about technology to be afraid of it (which is where most internal auditors are, as they focus on downside risk instead of upside value). Internal auditors must always be looking for ways to leverage technology for advantage
- Leverage the technology and systems that the organization and its management use to run the business. I don't understand why internal auditors have to implement their own reporting tools when management already has something in place that can be used, perhaps with a little tweaking
- Share what it finds with management
- Be willing to take chances to explore the potential for doing things different

I talked earlier about the use of gamification. Another new concept that might be useful is crowdsourcing.

One company was having difficulty with employees buying in to its code of conduct policy. There were complaints that it was onerous, not business-practical, and didn't always make sense. So they put a draft update to the policy out for comment and suggestion by every employee.

They made it clear that they wanted employees to suggest new wording, changes to policy, and so on. The employees responded with many comments and great ideas. The final document was embraced by the organization.

I can see how internal audit could share a risk and ask for ideas on how best to address it.

When it comes to new ideas, it is important to be open and receptive to any source. Managers with 20 years of experience don't have the insight into how new technologies like Pinterest could help internal audit. But a new intern might, even if they are not in internal audit.

11. **Where the CAE sends a message to the CEO asking to chat, and the CEO comes to the CAE's office.**

This happened to me at Maxtor. About 18 months after I joined, the CEO was replaced and the former chairman of the board, C.S. Park, took over. He was a very experienced former CEO who had led a larger company in the same business.

By then, I had built something of a reputation and C.S. had interviewed me when the board was debating whether the CEO was effective.

Even so, I was not prepared for the way in which C.S. (very soon after he became CEO) responded when I sent him an email asking for a few minutes to discuss a situation and get his input. Within five minutes, he was knocking at my door.

When internal audit is world-class, management is quick to make itself available every time the CAE calls.

First of all, the CAE has to know to ask for management time only when it is necessary, not just to chat about the weather. That way, calls from the CAE (and his direct reports) are known to be important to the manager.

Then the CAE has to make good use of his time with the executives. They are all immensely busy and their time is a scarce resource that needs to be respected by internal audit.

So say what needs to be said, confirm understanding, and leave.

I once gave a presentation at a risk management association conference. Afterwards, the president of the association asked to sit with me over lunch as he had a problem he thought I could help with.

He told me that while he reported directly to the CEO, he always found it difficult to get time with him. When he was able to arrange a meeting, the CEO seem to lack interest in what he was saying and was reluctant to act on his recommendations.

As this gentleman was speaking, I realized the problem. I didn't want to listen to him either, because he was boring! He spoke in a monotone without any passion in his voice, and used technical rather than business language.

If I didn't want to listen to him over lunch, how could I expect a busy CEO to want to listen?

When management doesn't find time to talk to you, or starts looking out the window as you are speaking, it's not a management problem. *You* are most likely the problem!

We need to talk in the language of the business about things that matter to the business, and make sure the individual we are talking to understands how they affect him.

We especially need to listen. People love people who listen to them, so try not to cut them off. Very often when managers talk and talk, they are talking about things we need to know – issues in running the business; risks we need to be aware of.

Management will open their calendars, minds, and ears to you when you constantly demonstrate that there is value for them in doing so.

12. **Expanding into new and cool stuff, even if not traditional audit areas, such as:**
    - **Process improvement**
    - **Six Sigma/Lean**
    - **Audits of risk management and governance processes**

At Solectron, the company decided that Lean Six Sigma would help drive down operating costs and increase both efficiency and quality. This was so important that it hired its new COO because he had a proven record of success with Lean Six Sigma as a GE executive.

They succeeded. Inventory was reduced while at the same time making the flow of materials to production faster and more efficient.

I attended Lean training myself. While I was never going to be a black belt, it at least gave me a basic understanding of the fundamentals. I sent each of my senior managers to training so they could not only talk the new language of the business, but use the techniques for operational auditing and so on.

By the way, Lean has now extended from its roots in Toyota Lean Manufacturing to Lean Finance.

Internal audit can use the concepts of Lean to ensure it is focused on quality product that is valued by its customers, eliminating every activity that does not add value as seen by its customers. I discuss this in my world-class auditing training. Much of what we spend time on, from time reporting to audit working papers, to audit report content that stakeholders don't need to hear, is waste – *muda* in the (Japanese) language of waste.

There are many risk areas where internal audit has rarely dared to go. Topics that we are only now starting to consider include risk management and governance processes.

I am not going to spend a lot of time on either – that would be another book of its own. But let me just say this:

- Effective risk management lets management and the board make far more intelligent decisions and have more confidence in running the business and taking risk, and improves both short and longer-term performance. How can we look ourselves in the mirror when we fail to tell the audit committee and top management that they are driving the company towards objectives without any visibility into the road ahead, its dangers and opportunities?
- A failure in governance (and this extends way beyond the code of conduct) can be enormously detrimental to organizational success Lord Smith of Kelvin chaired the UK's Smith Committee on Corporate Governance that provided guidance to audit committees. He told the IIA International Conference in Kuala Lumpur that "the fish rots from the head down". Should we not inform the audit committee when the executive team is fighting with the CEO or among themselves, or when we see that the CFO does not have the confidence of his team and peers?

13. **Where internal auditing is seen by management as a competitive advantage.**

In Chapter 22, I told the story about how Dwight Wiggins told the Governor of the state of New Jersey that internal audit gave Tosco a competitive advantage.

Why is this not a common occurrence?

If internal audit adds value to the organization, and world-class internal audit teams add far more than others, shouldn't the organization therefore have a competitive advantage.

I believe this to be the case although it is not often recognized either by the CAE or his customers.

Why can't the CAE shoot for the moon, where the value of internal audit (which includes all the informal consulting and advice it offers) is so great that it is seen as an advantage in the market?

Risk management functions are sometimes held out that way. It is time for internal audit to join them in the limelight.

14. **Where the CAE is never satisfied.**

OK, you and your team have been recognized as adding huge value and being world-class.

Do you stop there, confident and happy in your success?

No. What is world-class for your organization today may be insufficient for tomorrow.

The CAE should have a thirst for change and growth. Learn not only from other internal audit leaders and what they do well. Learn from leaders of other organizations entirely, like Marketing and Sales.

I like to read magazines like *Fast Company* because they profile innovative and creative thinkers in all walks of life. Maybe what works for them could, with some tailoring, work for me. At least it might stimulate me to think about something I had never thought about before. It might stimulate me to challenge what had worked for me in the past.

Innovative leaders think outside the box. They create something that excels and they love it. They love it so much it becomes a box for them and limits their ability to discard it in favor of something new.

We should not only think out of the box, but stay out of the box, and kick it as soon as somebody builds one.

Chapter 37: Celebrating mistakes

No, I don't open a bottle of champagne every time I or a member of my team makes a mistake.

But I believe that we should not live in fear of making a mistake, nor allow our team to fear our wrath if they fail for any reason.

Everybody should be forgiven a mistake. Its making repeated mistakes that worries me.

It's the failure to learn from your mistakes that becomes an issue.

I have made more mistakes than I can recall, and far more than I am willing to write about here.

Some I am willing to accept and live with.

For example, I know that I am slow to take disciplinary action. This has burned me on more than one occasion. When the individual didn't improve, their impact on the organization sometimes became more significant and the action I had to take more painful.

But, I am willing to accept that weakness. I am not the kind that pulls that trigger lightly and then can carry on as if nothing happened. I care about all my people and don't want to change who I am.

The first time I participated in a termination procedure was at Coopers in Los Angeles. All the secretaries reported to the group manager's assistant (Irene). But I was assigned a lady to handle most of my work. She was not doing very well.

Irene took control.

She talked to HR and then instructed my secretary to meet her in the conference room. I was "asked" to attend.

Irene calmly laid out the facts, informed the lady that her performance was not acceptable, and asked if I had anything to add. I did not.

She then asked my assistant if there was anything she wanted to say. There was:

> "I was wondering what was taking you so long."

I was so relieved I can remember how I went from sadness and guilt to acceptance and relief.

∞

I also can be impatient, especially with incompetence. My reaction can be thoughtless anger. That, in turn, can lead to damage to relationships, inappropriate actions, and so on.

Because I recognize this weakness, I have had to make adjustments.

The first is to acknowledge that what at first appears to be negligence or incompetence may not in fact be so. Perhaps the individual was not trained (for example, in completing computer ICQs) or provided the information they need to do their job. It may not be a failure of theirs but of their manager or employer.

Sometimes, I am wrong and they are right.

Then I also need to stop before reacting. Some say you should count to ten, but I am not always that disciplined. I can at least pause so I don't say what jumps into my mouth.

Shortly after I joined Maxtor, I was in Singapore and attended the opening meeting with the PwC audit team. The management team and I arrived in the conference room a few minutes early and then had to wait quite a while for the external auditors.

We were talking about the possible reasons for their late arrival when I heard a booming voice.

> Norman!!!!!!

I looked around.

I saw a grey-haired Asian gentleman with a grin the size of the moon racing towards me.

Who was he?

He reached me and grabbed my hands, shaking them vigorously while repeating my name over and over.

I smiled back and shook his hands in return.

I knew that I have a poor memory for names, so I was not surprised not to remember his. I had trained myself to politely say that I had forgotten.

Teck Soon Chew, he proudly announced.

Huh?

He told me that he had worked with me for a few months at Coopers in London. I had even trained him in computer auditing.

Then it dawned on me. I smiled back.

Richard!

He gave me a look. "No, Teck Soon".

Recognition spread across his face and he told me the story.

When he arrived in England, he met with our CAG group manager, James Fanshawe. James asked his name and when he was told "Teck Soon" said that nobody could say let alone remember and spell such a name. He said "We will call you Richard."

I have never know Teck Soon by that name. I am now pleased to know both the fine gentleman and the name to use when I speak to him.

When something goes wrong, my response is always to question whether I did something wrong. Very often, even when my team has a problem

235

(such as when the Solectron team arrived in Penang to do the procurement audit) my first thought is that it was my fault. Some may consider that a weakness but I consider it a strength. Not only do I not blame others too quickly, but when I do make a mistake I have learned to accept it, learn, and move forward.

As auditors, we need not only to accept the fact that we make mistakes and forgive ourselves, but that management makes honest mistakes as well. They should be given the same credit we give ourselves.

Let them learn from their mistakes so they can succeed and help the organization succeed.

Chapter 38: Looking back and forward

Internal audit has made great strides since I first became a CAE in 1990.

We have moved the edge of the practice from controls auditing to assurance over governance, risk, and control processes.

The majority of CAEs now report directly to the audit committee with functional reporting to at least the CFO if not the CEO.

But that leading edge is a thin one.

Far too few internal audit departments assess and provide assurance on the effectiveness of risk management.

Even fewer consider the risks of failures in governance programs and processes and include related engagements in their audit plan.

As I travel around the world, talking to internal auditors from Malaysia to Ottowa, I find a consistent pattern of growth. But, there remain pockets where the internal auditor is only there so that management can "check the box". This seems especially true in government (from local to national), where internal audit departments are upgraded or disbanded based on politics – a concept I find abhorrent in what should be an independent and objective function.

Part of the problem is that audit committees don't understand the potential of internal audit – and too many CAEs are not educating them. So, they don't demand more and too many CAEs are satisfied doing what is expected without trying to change and upgrade those expectations.

Still, I expect that internal auditing practices will continue to improve. Organizations need them, as PwC says, to move to the "next platform" and provide assurance that is not just about what used to be the risks, but what they are now and will be in the near future.

Our business environment is becoming more complex, more dynamic, and changing at an accelerating speed. I expect that internal audit leaders will risk to the challenge.

Those that do will create a competitive advantage for their organizations.

Acknowledgments

The number of people that have influenced my professional growth, both those for whom I worked and those who were on my team, is huge. I have tried to create a list, but know that I have forgotten many names. I hope they will forgive the omission.

Alan Marcum	Dave Wagner	Jarlath O'Neil-Dunne
Alan Proctor	David Clark	Jay Allen
Ann Tritsch	Debra Davies	Jean-Francois Heitz
Audrey Lee	Derek James	Jeff Mullis
Beate Morrow	Diana Marks	Jennifer Busch
Ben Washington	Dick Leonard	Jeremy Hacking
Benjamin Chiang	Don Hayes	Jim Cleary
Bill Baker	Don Villa	Jim Tolonen
Bob Broderick	Duston Williams	Joe Ingrassia
Bob Di Giorgio	Dwight Wiggins	Joe Johnson
Bob Lavinia	Ed Hajim	Joe Tang
Brian Jenkins	Frank Jastrob	Joe Throckmorton
Bridget Timberlake	Frederic Cordel	John Schwarz
Bruce Taylor	Gary Campanella	Joyce Lang
Cary Morgan	Gary Canady	Judy Kershaw
Charles Luellen	George Hermann	Julio Leung
Charlie Clegg	Gerry Ziolkowski	Kathleen Mack
Cheng Sim Meng	Ginger Doherty	Kathryn Munro
Chester Lin	Glenn Davis	Kathy Sanborn
Chris Lowe	Gordon Dow	Katie Vo
Christine Toh	Graeme Hopgood	Keith Budge
Clarence Frame	Greg Myers	Ken Ebbage
Clive Malcolm	Hazel Lau	Kevin Gilbert
Connie Chapman	Heinz Fridrich	Kiren Patel
CS Park	Houston Flournoy	Kurt Lauk
Dan Griedl	Ian Brown	Larry Geiger
Daryl Graham	Ivy Yeo	Laura (Morton) Nathlich
Dave Kovarik	James Fanshawe	LeRoy Larson
Dave Peterschmidt	Jan-Jan Wu Gross	Loretta Forti-Corson

Lorie Reynolds	Norman Miller	Soo Wai Mun
Lynn Bruneau	Norman Stratton	Stanley Halper
Mario Antoci	Osamu Yamada	Steve Costa
Mario Palencia	Patrick Sheehan	Steve Johnson
Mark Aurelius	Paul Low	Steve Wozniak
Marshall Johnson	Peter Schlesiona	Suzanne Pesko
Marty Patton	Peter Scott	Tabitha Gallo
Marty Ziomek	Phil Burbach	Tan Wee Liat
Mary Ann De Leon	Phil Cotton	Tan Yee Lin
Mary Anne Marks	Randy Saylor	Teo Han Kheng
Mary Beth Pastore	Richard Busch	Tim Cox
Mary Reis	Rich Schmidt	Tom Farrell
Matt Melone	Rick Allen	Tom Wisniewski
Michael Tennenbaum	Rick Klaus	Tony Gooey
Michal Brooding	Rick Teubner	Valerie Uyeda
Mike Guadagno	Rod Perry	Vic Pacheco
Mike Jacobs	Roger Herd	Wai Lim
Mike Ketchum	Ron Reed	Warren Androus
Mike Passaretti	Rosnah Ismail	Warren Ligan
Mike Wilmouth	Salman Qayyum	Wayne Budd
Mollie Bickerstaff	Shelly Hobbs	Wes Scott
Nancy Bush	Sofia Goh	Will Helton

With the Maxtor team

From left to right: Tan Yee Lin, guest from IT, Teo Han Kheng, Lorie Reynolds, Norman Marks, James Nguyen, Peter Schlesiona, Lee Ann Fennel (a guest from IT), Mike Guadagno, guest from IT, Rosnah Ismael, Katie Vo

The Business Objects Team

From left to right: Cary Morgan, Tabitha Gallo. Frederic Cordel, Olivier Delisle, Sophia Goh, Ian Brown, Katie Vo, Norman Marks, Chris Mehnert, and Lorie Reynolds

A proud moment: I receive the IIA's 2004 Thurston Award from IIA chairman Bob McDonald for the best article published that year in the *Internal Auditor* magazine. I was fortunate to receive the same award ten years later in 2014.

About the Author

Norman Marks, CPA, CRMA is an evangelist for "better run business", focusing on corporate governance, risk management, internal audit, enterprise performance, and the value of information. He is also a mentor to individuals and organizations around the world.

Norman was the chief audit executive of major global corporations for twenty years and is a globally-recognized thought leader in the professions of internal auditing and risk management. In addition, he has served as chief risk officer, compliance officer, and ethics officer, and managed what would now be called the IT governance function (information security, contingency planning, methodologies, standards, etc.) He ran the Sarbanes-Oxley Section 404 (SOX) programs and investigation units at several companies.

He is the author of the Institute of Internal Auditors' "Management's Guide to Sarbanes-Oxley Section 404: Maximize Value Within Your Organization"), which has been described as "the best Sarbanes-Oxley 404 guide out there for management", and "How Good is your GRC? Twelve Questions to Guide Executives, Boards, and Practitioners".

Norman is a member of the review boards of several audit and risk management publications (including the magazines of ISACA and the IIA), a frequent speaker internationally, the author of multiple award-winning articles, and a prolific blogger about better run business (consistently rating as one of the top global influencers in social media on the topics of GRC, internal audit, risk management, and governance).

Norman was profiled in publications of the AICPA and the IIA as an innovative and successful internal auditing leader. He has also been honored as a Fellow of the Open Compliance and Ethics Group for his GRC thought leadership, and as an Honorary Fellow of the Institute of Risk Management for his contributions to risk management.

Printed in Great Britain
by Amazon